Tales of the Norse Gods and Heroes

EDWARD THOMAS

DOVER PUBLICATIONS, INC.
Mineola, New York

Bibliographical Note

This Dover edition, first published in 2006, is an unabridged republication of *Norse Tales,* published by Oxford University at Clarendon Press, Oxford, 1921.

International Standard Book Number: 0-486-44939-4

Manufactured in the United States of America
Dover Publications, Inc., 31 East 2nd Street, Mineola, N.Y. 11501

PREFACE

THESE stories are taken from poems in the Old Norse tongue. They are the work of men who were perhaps for the most part Christians, living in the ninth and tenth centuries amidst a still keen aroma and tradition of Paganism. Their names have been lost, their poems confused and mutilated, in the course of a thousand years. Even the land where they wrote is unknown, and scholars have tried to discover it from the nature of the landscape and the conditions of life mentioned in the poems. For example, the editors of the *Corpus Poeticum Boreale* ask, 'Where could those curious mythologic fancies, which created Valhalla, and made of Odin a heavenly Charlemagne, which dreamed, like Cædmon, of the Rood as a tree that spread through the worlds, which pictured the final Doom as near, and nursed visions of an everlasting peace, holier even than Cynewulf's Phoenix figures—where could such ideas as these, alien as they are to the old Teutonic religion and ritual and thought, have been better fostered than in the British Isles, at a time when the Irish Church, with her fervent faith, her weird and wild imaginings, and curious half-Eastern legends, was impressing the poetic mind on one side, while the rich and splendid court of Eadgar or Canute would stimulate it on the other?' For the dates of the poems certainly fall within the period when the Northmen were plundering or colonizing the British and Irish coasts, and the Irish influence on the poets, as well as some Irish blood in their veins, seems unquestionable.

These tall, fair-haired Norsemen or Northmen were cousins of the Saxon conquerors of Britain, and followed soon after them in a wilder career of conquest. They fought and won treasure or land in every part of the West that could be reached by sea. Before the end of the eighth century they first reached our islands, and at the end of the twelfth were still raiding them. What the horse was to the Huns, said Cardinal Newman, the ship was to the Norsemen. From the glens and fiords of Scandinavia they scattered themselves on all the coasts of the Atlantic and the North Sea, the Mediterranean and the Black Sea, instigated by poverty, civil war, tyranny, or famine, at home, and a spirit of adventure. They fought Christians and Moslems. They settled in France, in Sicily, in Ireland, in Iceland, and Greenland. Some of them in the eleventh century sailed far into the south and discovered a country where the vine grew wild, and they called it Wineland and brought home from it grapes and vine wood. Others sought for Wineland in vain, and no one can say what land it was. The Norsemen gave England kings like Sweyn and Canute. They are remembered in Irish tales as the men of Lochlann. They burned the cathedral at St. Davids. Their writing upon the lion at the entrance to the arsenal at Venice can be seen to-day. Their blood is in the soil and in the veins of all the nations of the West.

The tales in this book were told by their poets in the years of their triumph, in the ninth, tenth, eleventh, and twelfth centuries, when the heroes in the tales were so real to them that one of their great men, Olaf the White, who was king at Dublin, was said to be descended from Sigurd and Brynhild. But already the tales were old, some unfathomably old. 'As one goes through the poems one is ever and anon face to face with a myth of the most childish and barbaric type—the world a giant, slain by the gods, who made heaven out of his skull, sun and moon from his eyes, earth out of his flesh, ocean out of his blood, clouds out of his brains, dwarfs out of the worms that bred in his body, and so on—a story that carries one back to pre-Aryan days, and must, one would fancy, have rather suited the imagination of the Ivernian thrall than of his Celtic lord, or his Scandinavian conqueror.

'Another almost as archaic is the early myth of the holy cow—firstborn of things, a figure common to Indian and Teutonic fancy. But side by side with these old outcrops of primaeval granite rock come the latest stratum, a wholly new system of beliefs, coloured through and through with Christian ideas—a heaven with a supreme God, angels, demons, a Holy Tree, a Hell, and a Doomsday. . . .'

The Gods in these poems still bear the title of Gods, unlike those in the Celtic stories. Yet they are not always more godlike. True, they are said to be all but omnipotent and all but immortal. At the same time one poem shows a mighty God unable to punish an impudent ferryman because the fellow is on the opposite side of a river.

Most of the stories of the Gods in these anonymous and fragmentary poems were gradually collected and para-phrased in a series of prose stories, interspersed with quotations from the poems. This collection, made in the thirteenth century by Snorri Sturleson, is known as the Prose Edda or Younger Edda, to distinguish it from the original group of poems called the Edda, or the Elder or

Poetic Edda. The first part of this book is a rearrangement of the Prose Edda, with several additional stories and considerable amplification of the dialogue-form and the character of Gangler. These myths do not represent, so far as we know, the whole of the belief of pagan Norsemen, nor is it likely that any one Norseman or group of Norsemen ever worshipped all those Gods together or kept in their mind a system such as the Prose Edda suggests. The collection is no more than a compilation of all that could be found, or all that was interesting when found, by a learned Christian, centuries after the conversion of the Norsemen.

The stories of the heroes in the second part of this book are taken from poems written in the same great period. They also are old stories. The different poets tell them in their own ways, one often inventing or presenting scenes and characters incompatible with those in another's poem. All of these stories of Sigmund, Helgi, and Sigurd are to be found—text, translations, notes, and introductions—in the '*Corpus Poeticum Boreale* (The Poetry of the Old Northern Tongue from the earliest times to the thirteenth century)', edited by Gudbrand Vigfusson and F. York Powell.

As many of the mythological stories were collected in the Prose Edda, so were the heroic in the prose story of the family of King Volsung, called ' Volsunga Saga.' The heroic tales are also used, much changed and amplified, by the anonymous German poet of the Nibelungen Lied, who inspired the most famous of the music dramas of Wagner. Both the early poems and the ' Volsunga Saga ' have been used in this second part.

CONTENTS

I. THE GODS

II. THE VOLSUNGS

THE GODS

I

THE MAKING OF THE WORLDS, OF GODS, AND OF GIANTS

Long ago, in Iceland, there was a king named Gangler who was famous for wisdom and for magic, and there were few things which he could not understand. One thing alone always astonished him, and that was the fact that whatever the Gods willed came to pass. He did not know whether this was due to their own great wisdom or to that of some even mightier Gods whom perhaps they themselves worshipped as men did them. This question returned to his mind again and again, even when he was old.

One day while the king was thinking about this power of the Gods he rode far away from his palace without looking at the road, and leaving his horse, which was a new one, to take him wherever it pleased. For he was thinking very hard. He did not know even that he was hungry. He did not know that what he was seeing was not the things around him, but those in his own brain. He was thinking about the Gods and their palace of Asgard, and he could see them as plain as his own warriors and his own house ; in fact the Gods were very much like his warriors, and the palace of Asgard very much like his house, except that they were larger and looked as if they must last for ever. It was not until the horse stumbled that he saw anything else but Gods

and Asgard. He slid gently off on to the ground, and
the young horse, glad to be free, walked on, turned round,
and galloped away.

As Gangler followed the horse with an indifferent eye
he saw that he was far up on the side of a stony mountain. It seemed as huge as the sky, especially as the
pale stones scattered about it resembled the flocks
of white clouds when those flocks are at their smallest
and highest in the blue. Though he had never before
been on this mountain or any like it, he was in no way
surprised or alarmed. It was, in fact, just such a mountain as he had been seeing with his mind's eye for some
time. At the top of it was a palace such as he imagined
the Gods' palace of Asgard to be. With untired step
he went on up the slope towards it. It did not seem
to him a wonderful thing that he should have come in
this short time to Asgard.

The first thing he saw was a mansion huge as a hill,
roofed with golden shields instead of tiles; and a man
stood at the entrance tossing up and catching seven
swords to amuse himself.

'What is your name?' said the man. 'Gangler,'
said he; 'I have come a long way and should be glad
of a night's lodging. Pray tell me whose house this is.'
'It is the king's,' said the man, and led him into the hall.
He saw room after room, and many people in them,
some drinking, some at play, others fighting. He went
without fear, yet very carefully, through the crowd, from
room to room, until he came to one where he saw three
thrones one above the other, and three crowned men
like brothers sitting on the thrones. 'Who are these?'
asked Gangler. 'The one on the lowest throne is a king,
and his name is Har; the second is equal to him, and
is called Jafnhar; the highest is Thridi, and he also is

a king.' Now Har himself spoke to Gangler, asking his
errand and telling him that all strangers were welcome
to eat and drink in his hall. ' But first,' said Gangler,
' I should be glad to know if there is any one here famous
for wisdom.' Har smiled : ' Unless you show yourself
the wisest, O man, I fear you may not return in safety.
Stand below, and here sits one who will be able to
answer your questions.'

Gangler bent down before the lowest of the thrones
and began to ask his questions.

' Who is the first or eldest of the Gods ? ' he asked.

' All-Father,' answered Har, in a voice like thunder,
' but he has twelve names.'

' Where is this God? what is his power, and what are
his works ? '

' He has been from the beginning,' answered Har,
' he reigns everywhere : all things obey him.'

And Jafnhar said in a voice like the sea : ' He made
heaven and earth and air, and all that dwells in them.'

Thridi also spoke, and his voice was like wind in
the forest : ' He made man, and gave him a soul that
cannot die.'

' But where,' asked Gangler, ' where was this God
before he made heaven and earth and air ? '

' He was with the Frost Giants,' said Har.

' And what was before that ? ' continued Gangler.

' In the beginning,' said Har, ' there was no earth,
no sea, and no heavens. There was no grass ; there was
nothing but a yawning chasm such as no man can
imagine and such as would make the Gods dizzy even
to think of.'

' Long before the earth,' said Jafnhar, ' a cloud world
was made, called Niflheim, a cold world of everlasting
fog, rain, and sleet.'

At these words Gangler felt himself upon a ship, as once he was in his younger days, sailing over an unknown sea after a storm. He saw before him the dim rocks and the dim marshland on the shore of an island where he could find no men, and nothing alive but sea-birds all crying together as they flew round about in the mist. It was between a wet autumn and a bitter winter. The coast of that uninhabited island seen through the sea-spray, the mist, and the low grey clouds must have been like Niflheim. He remembered yet another scene. He had just stepped out of his house after a night of rain and wind. The rain and the wind had beaten round the walls all night, so that as he lay awake, the only man awake in his hall, he seemed to be on a ship. And as he stepped out in the morning he thought at first that he was in the middle of the sea. Below him was the steep hill on the top of which stood his house, but the hill was blotted out by mist. Through the mist he could see mountains which he had never seen before, but either they, or he and the house, were moving. He dared not take another step lest he should fall into that strange sea. Then as he stood still thinking, he saw that the mountains were clouds. His house and the little piece of ground where he was standing seemed to be all that was left of the earth. The night's storm had washed away all the rest, and there he was ship-wrecked in a sea of clouds and mist, rocking and swirling round about. This sea must have been like Niflheim.

'But before Niflheim,' said Thridi, not noticing Gangler, ' there was a world in the south called Muspell-heim. It is a flaming and burning world, too bright and too hot for any one, man or god, who was not born there. It is guarded by one with a flaming sword seated at its border. His name is Surtur, and at the end of the world he will go forth with his flaming sword and harry and overcome the Gods and burn the world.'

' Tell me more,' said Gangler, ' of the chasm between this burning world and Niflheim.'

Thridi answered him : ' One half of the chasm was fog and frost from Niflheim, the other bright because of the sparks and flakes of fire of Muspellheim ; and in the middle part the frost was melted and the drops of the vapour rising from it grew into the shape of a man. This was Ymir, the ancestor of all the Frost Giants.'

Where did he live ? ' asked Gangler, ' and how did he live ? '

' A cow also was made out of the drops of the melted frost,' said Har, ' and four rivers of milk flowed from her teats, and Ymir lived on the milk.'

' What did the cow feed on ? '

' The cow fed on the salty hoar-frost that she licked from the stones. At the end of the first day hair like a man's appeared on the stone that she had licked ; at the end of the second there was a man's head ; on the third the complete likeness of a man. He was fair to see, big and strong, and his name was Buri. He begot a son named Bor. This son begot three sons, Odin, Wili, and Wé. These were Gods.'

' And how did the sons of Ymir agree with the sons of Bor ? '

' The sons of Bor,' said Har, 'slew the Giant Ymir, and his blood drowned all his children except one called Bergelmi, who saved himself and his wife in an ark. The gods made the earth out of Ymir's body in the midst of the chasm. His flesh was the land, his bones the mountains, his blood the sea.'

Here Jafnhar spoke : ' The blood ran out of his

wounds in a great ring encircling the earth. On the shore of this ocean dwell the Giants.'

' Ymir's skull,' said Thridi, ' made the heavens above the earth. They set a Dwarf at each of the four quarters, North, South, East, West. With the sparks and flakes of fire scattered from Muspellheim they made stars to move in the heavens, to give light, and to mark the days and nights, spring and summer, autumn and winter.'

' Do the Giants not seek revenge ? '

' They are kept out by a great wall,' said Har. ' Inside this wall is Midgard, the abode of men.'

' But where did men come from to dwell in Midgard? '

' As they were walking on the sea-shore, these sons of Bor found two trees, and taking them up made them into men. Odin gave them breath and life, Wili gave them the power to know and to move, Wé gave them speech, hearing, and sight. They gave them also clothes and names. The man was called Ash and the woman Elma, and these two were the first parents of all mankind living in Midgard. Then the Gods made an earthly city for themselves called Asgard, in the centre of Midgard but high above the homes of men. Highest of all in Asgard is the solitary seat of Odin, called Lidskialf. From there he can see all the world and all that men are doing therein. One of Odin's names is King of Lidskialf. Odin and Frigga, his wife, are parents of all the Gods. Rightly, therefore, is Odin named All-Father.'

For a little time Gangler was silent. Then suddenly he asked : ' What is Night ? '

' Night,' said Har, ' is a Giant's daughter, and like all of them she is dark. She married one of the Gods, and they had a son whose name was Day. This child

was as bright and beautiful as his father. Odin took
him and his mother Night, and gave them two chariots
and two horses, and gave them the heavens to drive in,
first one and then the other. Night's horse is Rimfaxi;
when he has run his course he stands still, champing the
bit; his mouth is covered with foam and this falls to
the earth, where men call it dew. Skinfaxi is Day's
horse, and as he runs light is shaken out of his mane
over earth and the heavens.'

' And who guides the sun and the moon ? '

' Once there was a man who had two children so
beautiful that he called them Sun and Moon. This
angered the Gods, and they snatched up the two children
and set them in the cars of the sun and moon to guide
them across the sky for ever—until Ragnarok.'

Gangler had never heard the word Ragnarok. If he
thought at all about it, he supposed it was only a muttering, an oath of some sort, in the throat of Har. ' Why,'
he asked, ' does the sun always go on ? It is as if she
were flying in fear from some one.'

' She is in fear. Some one is pursuing her, and he is
not far behind.'

' Who is it ? '

' A wolf named Skoll, and one day he will catch her
and devour her. Another one named Hati follows the
moon and one day will devour him. They are two of
the children of the old giantess living in Iron Wood
on the east of Midgard. She has many children.'

Gangler thought for a little while of Iron Wood,
and an old Giantess with a beard there in the darkness,
and a herd of her children who were wolves, some of
them running out from under the trees of Iron Wood
to look at Midgard. Gangler had never seen Iron Wood,
but when Har spoke of it he saw clearly the edge of a

great wood. He was hunting a bear, and had left all his companions far behind; and it was the end of a winter's day. The bear had gone into that wood, and though he was not afraid yet he stood still, leaning upon his spear and looking at the wood. The trees were oak-trees, twisted, bare and black, and he could not see far into the wood. All was black except one tiny blot of orange on a low branch of one oak-tree. All was silent except one tiny song which came from that blot of orange. It was a robin singing, and he stood watching it. Nothing was moving inside the wood. Suddenly the light was gone, and the robin turned, flitted, and was silent. He watched for it, but in vain. Long after he had ceased to expect the bird or the song, he remained standing still with his eyes towards the forest of black oaks. It was useless now to follow the bear. Slowly he turned back and wearily retraced his steps, so that not until the night was half gone did he enter his house. Several times afterwards he turned the hunt that way in the hope of finding the forest and going into it. But he never could. Years went by, and he forgot the forest. Now he remembered it, and shuddered at the thought of the old Giantess and her wolf children that would some day devour the sun and the moon. It seemed to him that the oak forest where the bear had disappeared was Iron Wood.

II

HEAVEN AND EARTH; GODS, DWARFS, AND ELVES

WHEN he had come back from this wandering of his mind, Gangler tried to hide his thoughts by asking :

' Which is the road from earth to heaven ? '

Har laughed :

'Have you never been told how the Gods made a bridge from earth to heaven, called Bifrost ? You have seen it, if you did not know what it was. Perhaps you call it the rainbow. It is a most mighty bridge, and yet if—and yet when the sons of Muspellheim ride over it they will break it down.'

' The Gods cannot have made such a bridge in earnest. They might have made one that could not be broken down.'

' You are but a man. The Gods are not to blame, Bifrost is a good bridge. It is the best of all possible bridges ; it cannot resist the sons of Muspellheim, nor can anything else. Why, then, should the Gods have tried to make a better bridge, when they had made one which would keep out any one and anything save the sons of Muspellheim ? It keeps out the Giants.'

It would have been easy to annoy Har still more, but Gangler asked him :

' What did the All-Father make after Asgard ?

' He formed a council to govern Asgard and Midgard. They built themselves a temple of gold for the high seat of the All-Father and the twelve seats of the other

Gods. It is the best and the biggest house on earth, and its name is Gladsheim. They built another beautiful palace, called Wingolf, for the Goddesses. They built also a smithy, and there they worked at the forges with hammer and tongs. They made things of metal and gems and wood, but above all they made things of gold. Everything in their houses was of gold, and this was called the age of gold. It was destroyed by the coming of women from Giantland.

'While they sat on their thrones the Gods remembered the maggots in the dead body of Ymir, and they gave them the shape and the understanding of men, and homes in the earth and in the rocks. These were the Dwarfs, and though small they had often much wit.

'At one time it happened that a Dwarf, named All-wise, took the shape and size of a God, and by a trick persuaded the Gods to promise him Freya for his wife. After giving orders to the servants to deck his cavern and make ready a feast for the bride, he hurried off merrily to fetch her home. He had now returned to his true shape, and outside Valhalla he was met by Odin, who said to him, seeing his wedding attire:

' " Who are you ? why are you pale about the nose ? You look a sorry sort of bridegroom."

' " My name is All-wise," answered the Dwarf. " My home is in a cave under the earth. I have only come here to fetch my bride, and I hope you are not thinking to break your promise."

' " But I am," said Odin, " I am the bride's guardian, and she can do nothing without my consent. I was not at home when she was betrothed."

' " Who are you, then, to be guardian to the lovely maid ? " asked the Dwarf, contemptuously.

' " I am the Wayfarer, Longbeard's son. Nevertheless,

the maid cannot make a match unless I consent," said Odin.

' " If that is so, I would rather have your permission, though you are a wayfaring man. I will not lose the snow-white maid by any scruples."

' " She shall be yours, All-wise, if you can answer all my questions. Tell me first, you who probably know everything, what other names has the Earth ? "

' " The Gods call it the ' Field '; Giants call it the ' Ever-green '; Elves the ' Growing '."

' " What are the names for Heaven ?"

' " Gods call it ' Warmer '; Giants ' High-home '; Elves ' Fair-roof '; Dwarfs ' Drip-hall '."

' " What are the names for the Moon ? "

' " It is the ' Whirling-wheel ' in Hell ; the ' Hastener ' among Giants ; ' Sheen ' among Dwarfs ; ' Year-teller ' the Elves call it."

' " And the Sun ? "

' " It is ' Dwales-doll ' among Dwarfs ; ' Ever-glow ' among Giants ; ' Fair-wheel ' among Elves."

' " What is the Wind ? "

' " It is the ' Waverer ' of the Gods ; the ' Whooper ' of the Giants ; the ' Soft-gale ' of the Elves ; in Hell they call it ' Whistle-gust '."

' " What is the Sea ? "

' " The Gods call it ' Level '; the Elves ' Sea-blink '; the Dwarfs ' Deep '."

' " And Fire ? "

' " It is called ' Greedy ' by Giants ; ' Furnace fire ' by Dwarfs ; in Hell it is the ' Destroyer '."

' " What is Night ? "

' " It is called ' Unlight ' by Giants ; ' Sleep-joy ' by Elves ; ' Dream-fairy ' by Dwarfs."

' " What is Ale ? "

' " ' Beer ' among Gods ; ' Clear-beer ' among Giants ;
' Mead ' in Hell ; ' Good cheer ' among Dwarfs."

' And thus by many questions, which could only be
answered after much thinking, Odin wasted the Dwarf's
time.

' " I never met one man," he said, " who knew so
many different names. But your wit has been too much
for you. The Sun is now up, or, as Dwarfs call it, the
' Dwales-doll ' ; and the Sun is too much for Dwarfs;
they cannot endure its light."

' The hall was full of sunshine, and All-wise was turned
to stone; and for a stone to marry a bride is impossible.'

' Which, then, is the chief abode or most holy place
of the Gods ? '

' Under the ash-tree, Yggdrasil. There they, hold their
court every day,' answered Har. ' Yggdrasil is the
greatest and best of trees. It stretches out over the world
as a common ash-tree does over a cottage. The roots
of it are in Heaven, in Giantland, and in Niflheim.
A dragon is always gnawing at the root which is in
Niflheim. Many other serpents also gnaw at the roots;
four harts nibble the buds ; and the bark is rotting.
An eagle who knows many things has its perch among
the branches of Yggdrasil, and a squirrel named Rata-
tusk runs up and down, telling the eagle's words to the
dragon and trying to make strife between them. Under
the root in Giantland is Mimir's brook, whose water
gives wisdom and understanding. The All-Father himself
once went to the brook for a draught, but Mimir would
not give it unless he left an eye for a pledge. Under the
third root is Weirds' brook, and beside it the Gods
sit in judgment. Every day they ride up over Bifrost
bridge to Weirds' brook. These are the names of their

horses : Gleed and Gylli, Gler and Skidbrim, Silvertop and Sini, Hostage and Fallow-hoof, Goldcrest and Lightfoot. Only one of the Gods may not ride over Bifrost, and that is Thor. If he were to ride over it in his thunder-chariot he would set it on fire. So he must walk, wading through the deep waters of Kormth and Wormth and the two Charlocks every day.

' Many fair palaces have been built in Heaven. One standing close to the Weirds' brook is the home of three maidens, Weird, Verdandi, and Skuld. These are the Norns; they water Yggdrasil with the water of Weirds' brook, and they make men's fates. They dwell alone except for two swans in the brook. There are many other Norns. One or another of them comes to every child that is born, and decides what is to be its fate. Such Norns are of the race of Gods. Some Norns belong to the race of Dwarfs, others are Elves. Of Elves there are two kinds. The Elves of Light, dwelling in Elflheim which is in Heaven, are as bright as if sunlight flowed in their veins for blood; but the Dark Elves who live down in the earth are blacker than pitch.'

Gangler hardly listened to this about the two sorts of elves. ' If these Norns,' he said to Har, ' give men their fates, good or bad, their gifts are very different. They are not like a good farmer who gives equally to his cattle that all may thrive, but like a bad mother who gives good things to one child and bad or nothing at all to another. Some men are fortunate and rich, others poor and in every way unfortunate ; some live to be old, others are cut off in childhood or in their prime.'

' Good Norns,' said Har, ' make good fates for men, but evil Norns make bad ones, and they alone should be blamed for them.'

Gangler was silent and not glad. He could see these

Norns too plainly to speak. They were three black-haired sisters living alone in a large dark house beside the brook. They never spoke to one another, but seemed to understand without speaking as they went to and fro in the long rooms, weaving. They wove just as if they were working at clothes for some one else. They had no joy in it, but went on and on. They did not care what they had made, when once it was done. They were like slaves who have too much work to do for a master whom they never see. One was as pale as any living thing can be, and sighed continually as she went from one web to another : she was too tired to leave off her toil. One of her sisters seemed to have more spirit, for now and then she clutched at the web and tore it in anger ; but she was angry with herself, not with what she had made, and so she began another immediately, and the only effect of her anger was that her hand trembled and her lips were touched with foam. The other was neither sad nor glad. She never smiled or sighed, but worked as if she were asleep. It was so easy to her that she closed her eyes. Yet, like her two sisters, she laid down her work at the very moment when her day was over, and never began before it was time. And as Gangler watched them he said to himself : ' If these three women make men's fates, somebody has made theirs for them long ago. If they were to die it would not be easy to find three other such sisters among the slave women who are no longer young.' But he was still silent.

Therefore Har continued :

' Many other fair mansions stand in heaven. There is Breidablik, and Glitnir, and three most beautiful of all, brighter than the sun, which will stand when heaven and earth pass away, and there in the glittering ale-hall under the golden roof built upon the hills of the moon just men shall dwell for ever. Some say that this is now the palace of the Elves of Light, but we do not know. We have only heard tell of it.'

Gangler was tired, and would have fallen asleep but for those three kings. To his half-dreaming eyes they seemed to be Gods. He was afraid that they would disappear if he slept, and that they might send him away if he asked no more questions. He asked, therefore, why it was that Summer was hot and Winter cold.

' A wise man,' said Har, ' would never ask that, and any foolish one can answer it. The reason is that the father of Summer was of a sweet and kindly nature, and Summer took after him ; while the father of Winter was grim and chill, and his son likewise.'

In spite of his fear and his good intentions, Gangler fell fast asleep while Har was speaking.

III

ODIN AND VALHALLA

As those three kings were still sitting on their thrones when he awoke, Gangler refreshed himself with food and drink before asking them further questions. First he asked:

' Who are the Gods that men must believe in ? '

' There are twelve,' answered Har.

' There are also the Goddesses,' said Jafnhar, ' no less divine and mighty.'

' The greatest of the Gods· is Odin. He is the God of men and of all other Gods, and the others obey him as children do their father. Frigga is his wife, a Goddess who sees all that is to happen in the future but never reveals it. Odin has many other names. He is called...'

Har rumbled out a long roll of half a hundred names for Odin. When he had come to an end, Gangler said:

' Odin has many names. Only a wise man can remember them all and know why each was given to the God.'

' Yes,' said Har, ' a man must have a good memory to remember these names. There is a good reason for them all. Each one was given because of some power which he possesses or some deed which he performed. There is nothing which he cannot do, and he does it better than it could be done by any other. He knows everything, and sees everything with the help of his two ravens, Hugin and Munin. They sit upon his shoulders and tell him all they have seen and heard in flying about the world. One of Odin's names is Friend of the Ravens.'

'Then he does not know and see everything by himself?' said Gangler.

'His task is not easy,' said Har. 'Much of his wisdom came from the precious mead which belonged to Balethorn's son. He learnt nine sage songs from this giant, but before he could do so he had to hang nine days and nights on the gallows without bread or wine, and wounded with a spear. It was not by lying at ease in Lidskialf that he became famous and earned the name of Dain among Elves, Dwale among Dwarfs, All-wise among Giants. He learnt songs such as no king's daughter or any son of man knows. They will cure all sorrow and all kinds of sickness. They will blunt an enemy's sword and make his chains drop from the captive. They will stop the arrow before it has reached its mark: they will save a man from all dangers. If a hall is aflame when men are asleep, one of the songs will stay it, be the flame never so broad. They will make wars to cease. They will quiet the sea. They will defeat witches. They will put breath into the dead. They will gain the love of a maid. But what these songs are Odin has kept secret save from Frigga, his wife.'

'How should I know him?' asked Gangler. 'What is he like?'

'No man was ever in doubt about Odin unless he disguised himself. He is tall and old, like an old king; but he will never be older, nor can he be wiser. He has but one eye, for the other he left with Mimir after drinking the wise water of Mimir's brook.'

But in spite of these words of Har, Gangler pictured Odin not as an old king, perhaps because he was an old king himself, but as an old wayfaring man whom he had once met in winter. He was half sitting, half standing against a bank, and appeared to be looking

earnestly up the road. The king thought he had never
seen a man look so wise and noble, and yet he could
not see his face at all, but only the big white beard
jutting out into the snow. His chin rested upon his
two hands, which were clasped on the handle of his long
walking-staff. He was grand enough to have been a king
of men, and yet he was clothed in the manner of a poor
wayfarer. His legs and head were bare. What was
strangest of all was that a raven had alighted on the top
of his head and stood there still. Evidently the man
was from some far-off country, yet the way he must have
come was over mountains impassable in that season even
to the shepherds of the country. He must have been
travelling for no common cause to have taken that short
but perilous cut. Or was it hunger only? For fear of
disturbing him, the king had stood still a few yards
off. He now moved forward to speak. The raven flew
in half a circle to the nearest tree. ' Where are you
bound, old man? ' asked the king. The man did not
move or speak. The king now went close up to him,
thinking he might be deaf. Then he saw that the old
man was dead. It was this wayfarer that he now saw
when Har spoke to him of Odin.

' One of the reasons why Odin has so many names,'
said Har, ' is that he has travelled far and seen many
peoples and had many adventures. Sometimes he took
another name to conceal his own, as when he visited
the Giant Wafthrudni.'

' What was that adventure? ' asked Gangler.

' One day when Odin was with Frigga, his wife, in
Valhalla, he told her that he was longing to visit Wafthrudni in Giantland, to see which could get the better
of the other in a trial of wit. Frigga urged him not to go,
because everybody said that the Giant was very wise.

Odin, however, had never seen him and was determined to go, now that his wife seemed to think the Giant might prove the wiser of the two. So he set out, and Frigga had nothing to do but wish him farewell and good fortune in Giantland.

'Odin greeted Wafthrudni, and said that he had come to see him and to learn if he were truly a wise and learned Giant. At this Wafthrudni was a little angry, and he said that the stranger should never leave the hall alive unless he showed himself the wiser of the two. He also asked Odin his name, and the God said that it was Ganger. He asked Ganger to come up and sit beside him, but he would not. Then Wafthrudni asked him many questions about things on earth and in heaven, and Odin answered them every one rightly. The Giant was astonished above all when the stranger was able to tell him the name of the plain where Surtur and the Gods are to meet for battle.

' "Thou art wise indeed, O Ganger," said the Giant. "Come now up to my bench and let us sit and talk together." He was glad to have so wise a guest, who answered swiftly and clearly.

'But now when Odin had sat down it was his turn to question. He asked about the beginnings of the world, the making of the earth and the Frost Giants, and who was the father of Winter and of Summer; and where the wind came from. Wafthrudni knew it all, yet he answered slowly, as if it had been long since he had had to show his knowledge and he hardly knew where to find it. At length Odin began to ask him about things that were to happen in the future. He asked where the new sun would come from after the wolf had swallowed this one up, and the Giant knew. He asked what kind of death Odin would have to die when the

end came, and the Giant told him that the wolf would
swallow up the All-Father also. Then Odin asked him,
" What did Odin whisper in his son Balder's ear when
Balder lay dead ? " Wafthrudni laughed and looked
craftily at Odin, saying, " What you whispered in your
son's ear long ago no one knows. Odin, it is vain for
me to strive with you in wit, wisest of all as you are and
ever shall be." Whether Odin did not altogether like
the words " ever shall be ", who shall say ? But he
and the Giant remained silent in the hall that evening,
nor could Frigga persuade her husband to tell her about
the contest on his return.

'Once Odin went as a blind wayfarer to the hall
of King Heidrek, who was a famous man for asking
and answering riddles. He thought little of the blind
man, and said that he would guess all his riddles or else
forfeit his life. Odin began asking riddles.

' " I wish," he said, " I had what I had yesterday.
Guess what it was : it harms men, hinders words, and
yet also rouses words ? "

' " Ale," said the king.

' " What is that one with a high voice, who walks on
hard places over and over again ; he kisses very fast,
has two mouths, and walks on nothing but gold ? "

' " A goldsmith's hammer," said the king.

' " What was that I saw outside the hall turning
its head down towards Hell and its feet up to the
sun ? "

' " A leek," said the king.

' " What is it that has ten tongues, twenty eyes, and
forty feet, and moves along ? "

' " A sow with a litter of nine pigs," said the king.

' " Who are the two that have ten feet, three eyes,
and one tail ? "

' " The One-eyed Odin riding Sleipnir, his eight-
legged horse."

' " What did Odin whisper in Balder's ear before he
was laid on the funeral pile ? "

' " That is what only I know besides Odin," said the
king, but as he would not answer he was beaten and
ought to have forfeited his life. Instead of giving in he
drew his magic sword and struck at Odin, who escaped
by flying away in the shape of a hawk. Heidrek did
not live long afterwards, but died by that very sword
in the hand of one of his slaves.

' At another time Odin went disguised to the hall of
King Geirrod, a wise and cruel king, but not wise
enough to see that the stranger was no common traveller.
He seized Odin, who made no resistance, and bound
him down on the hearth so that the fire scorched him.
For three days Geirrod left him there, refusing him food
and drink. At the end of the third day Agnar, the king's
son, took pity on him and gave him a horn full of wine
to drink, and as he lay there Odin burst out into a song.
First he hailed the good Agnar, saying, " The God of men
hails thee. Thou never gavest or shall give a more lucky
drink." Lying there on the hearth, he saw in vision the
Gods and the halls of Asgard, all bright and blessed in
their beauty like the white clouds shining high in the
air when the lower clouds are still ragged and dark after
a tempest. He sang of Valhalla and its five hundred
and forty doors, where every day came the men who
died in battle, made whole again and rejoicing in the
wine of Odin served by the Valkyries ; of Breidablik,
Balder's palace, the most blessed of palaces ; of the other
beauteous abodes ; of the tree Yggdrasil ; of the sun
rejoicing in the heavens, and of the wolf that follows it.
As sometimes a chump of old wood sings a bird-like

song before it catches fire on the hearth, and all men
become silent to listen to it, because it is winter and
all birds are songless; thus Odin sang on the hearth,
but far more sweetly and more mightily. Then even as
the chump of wood suddenly ends its song and bursts
into flames, so the God ceased and rose up, revealing
himself as the God above all other Gods. Geirrod tried
to rise up, but could not. Odin turned to him and spoke
in anger : " Geirrod, thou art drunk, thou hast drunken
too deep. Never shalt thou join the company of the
blessed ones who drink with Odin at Valhalla. Thou
shalt be a corpse, and no more. For I am Odin."
Once more Geirrod tried to rise up; he stumbled over
his sword, and it pierced him through the body so that
he fell dead; and the good Agnar became king and
reigned in his father's place.'

'Why are there five hundred and forty doors to
Valhalla ? ' asked Gangler.

'Because the host within could not break forth when
the day comes if there were fewer. In Valhalla Odin
gathers all the warriors who die in battle. In the end
they will go forth with Odin to fight at the day of
Ragnarok-Ragnarok. But until then they fight and
eat and drink and welcome the new-comers. By night
the shining of their swords lights up their feasts, and they
sleep like logs until the cock crows and it is time to begin
fighting again. No wounds can outlast that sleep. However much they gash and pierce one another they are
healed again as easily as linen is washed, and beautiful
Valkyries, who are Odin's cup-bearers, serve these chosen
ones also with drink. There is no end to the drink of
Odin. You could as soon use up all the light of the sun
as all his ale. For in the midst of the hall rises a great
ash, and there is a goat called Alidrun always nibbling

at the roots of the tree. Instead of milk, ale runs out of the udders of this goat all day into a jar that can never be emptied. Into this jar the Valkyries dip the horns and the goblets, and hand them to the warriors. For much fighting makes them thirsty, and much drinking makes them thirstier still. Nor does this spoil their appetites. Every day a boar of suitable size is boiled for them by Odin's cook. But just as the warriors grow no larger for all their enormous feasts, so the boar is no smaller by the end of the day. The boar will last as long as Valhalla.'

' Do they never grow weary ? ' asked Gangler.

' They do not,' said Har, ' or what good would it do them to go to Valhalla ? It would be better for them to be as dead as Geirrod. No. They are never weary. But of course they grow tired at times, and very glad they are, because if they did not they would never have the pleasure of resting. They have no enemies in Valhalla. When the young King Helgi died, that was like a noble ash among thorn-bushes, he entered Valhalla ; and the first man he saw was his old enemy, King Hunding; and he said, " Hunding, pray get ready a bath and light a fire and tie up the hounds and bait the horses, and give the hogs their swill before thou goest to sleep ! " Helgi did not know yet that he was in Valhalla. Then Hunding rose up and greeted him, and they sat down together. In Valhalla men never think of yesterday or to-morrow. They do not begin a fight with thinking of the end of it. They do not spoil one mouthful of the boar by considering the next or the last. They eat because Odin has given them teeth, stomachs, appetites, and a huge wild boar. They drink for an equally good reason. No man could refuse drink offered to him by one of the Valkyries.

'The Valkyries are sisters of the Norns. Some of them have been Norns, and some of them may be Norns again. But in Valhalla these maids of Odin are not sad ; nor do they think about men's fates. They are beautiful, and they serve Gods and men. They are almost as tall as a warrior, so that the eye of a warrior standing up is on a level with the tops of their heads ; sitting down, his eye is level with their girdles. As they go to and fro their long yellow hair streams behind them ; for their steps are swift, and the wind blows without ceasing through the five hundred and forty doors. They stop often to talk to the warriors. - Their voices are very sweet, and they are wise with such wisdom as is necessary in Valhalla. Sometimes Odin sends one of them down to the battle-field to summon a dying warrior to the banquet : after some battles more than one of the Valkyries have been seen, sitting on horseback like warriors, with helms and shields. Dying men have heard them speak to one another about the dead who have gone to increase Odin's host in Valhalla. King Hakon talked to one of them as he lay dying on the deserted battle-field ; but very soon she had to leave him, saying : " But now we must ride to the great city of the Gods, to tell Odin that a mighty king is coming to see him." Some newly dead warriors will hardly believe that they are in Valhalla until they see the Valkyries. When King Hakon arrived, Odin sent two of the Gods out to lead him into the hall. Hakon was dripping with blood ; he was angry, and would not notice the kind words of the messengers, though they bade him take ale with the Gods and join his eight brothers who were already there. He would not take off his armour, but said to himself : " One should take good care of one's helm and mail-coat. 'Tis good to have

things ready at hand." But as he said this he went
in at one of the doors. As he saw the Valkyries serving
the warriors, he thought no more about the old hacked
mail-coat and the broken helmet. Their beauty made
him glad.

'Yet some tell that they have seen Valkyries on the
battle-field, weaving a red web of fate as they rode in
and out among the hosts. They were singing a wild song
about this web. They were weaving it, they said, as
friends of Odin. They could order the battle; they
could choose the victors; they sang as the battle drew
to an end; their web covered both sky and earth
blood-red. They had destroyed their enemies and
saved their friends, and they rode away fast on their
bare-backed steeds, with their drawn swords in their
hands.'

IV

BALDER AND LOKI

GANGLER was now anxious to hear more about Balder,
so he said to Har :

'Why should Odin whisper in his son's ear when he
was dead ? '

'No God was so much loved either by Gods or by
men as Balder. He was also the most beautiful; his
nature was happy and strong, and his beauty shone out
like the sun. Some said that he looked too like a woman,
and they laughed at him for it unless they happened to
know the weight of his fist. Yet he was both mild and
wise. Nothing dark or evil could exist near him or
in his radiant palace, Breidablik. Only in his sleep
could evil come to Balder, and at length it came. He
dreamed evil dreams, so that when he awoke he was sad,
though he could not remember them. The Gods were
sad at the sight of Balder haunted by dreams, and they
took counsel in order to find out, if possible, why the
dreams came. But Odin himself went alone down to
Niflheim to see a prophetess and ask her about Balder.
The ancient sire of the Gods laid the saddle on his horse
Sleipnir, and rode down until he came to the lofty hall
of Hell. At the gate stood a huge burial-mound which
had been raised over the body of the prophetess. There
he stopped, and began chanting spells to raise her from
her grave. Suddenly, where there had been nothing
a moment before, there was the prophetess, asking :

' " Who is this stranger that has made me take this

weary journey up from the dead ?   I have been snowed,
on with snow; I have been beaten with much rain ;
I have been drenched with dew ; long have I been dead."
　‘ Then Odin said :
　‘ " My name is Vegtam the Traveller. Tell me news
of Hell, and I will tell thee news of Earth. Is there any
one for whom they are getting ready the benches for
a banquet in Hell ? "
　‘ " Yes," answered the prophetess, " they are getting
ready for Balder in Hell, though in their palace the Gods
are merry and not thinking of such things. But I have
already said more than I meant."
　‘ " Oh ! speak on, wise one, I pray thee; I must know
everything now. Who will be the death of him ?
Who will slay Odin's son, Balder ? "
　‘ " It will be Hod. He shall slay his brother. I will
speak no more."
　‘ " But thou must, O prophetess. Tell me at least
who are these wailing maidens that I see, three of them
casting up their arms in sorrow ? "
　‘ Then she laughed the laugh of the dead, for she knew
that Odin alone could see these things. She bade him
ride home, and said that no one should see her again until
the Destroyers came at the end.
　‘ But while Odin was away Frigga had been thinking
how to save Balder, if it was death that was haunting
his dreams. She made everything in earth and air and
water, and fire itself, take an oath not to harm Balder.
This they all gladly did. There was now great rejoicing
among the Gods, first, because Balder was safe ; and
second, because they had invented a new game. The
game was to throw all kinds of weapons at Balder, to
show that metal, wood, or stone would do him no
harm. Balder stood up without flinching while they

threw javelins and stones, cut with swords and axes, thrust with lances, battered with clubs. Balder was unhurt, and all were laughing with gladness and amusement. It was thought a great honour to Balder to show him thus how nothing would consent to hurt him, not even the sharp edges and points that were made to do harm. Only one God, Loki, was sorry that the sword would not cut Balder, nor the javelin pierce him, nor the stones bruise his flesh.'

'Why was that?' asked Gangler. 'Was there a quarrel between Balder and Loki?'

'No.'

'Then why was Loki sorry that he could not be hurt?'

'Because it was his nature.'

'I see,' said Gangler. For he really did see, as soon as Har spoke, a crooked-bodied and crooked-minded God, in his mind's eye. This was Loki. Except that he was mightier than any man, he was made exactly in the image of a man whom Gangler had known long before. He was the fool at a king's court. His face had made every one laugh since he was a little boy, and so the king took him for his fool. Every one continued to laugh at whatever he said because he had a ridiculous face. Often he said very wise things, and often very cruel and strange things, but they laughed all the same. The fact is that he made them all into such fools with laughter that they could not judge between wisdom and folly. He himself never laughed, because he knew that if ever he did they would look very grim and think that he was laughing at them. But his mouth curled and twitched, and they laughed all the more. Loki's mouth was curling and twitching when Gangler saw him, and all the Gods roared with laughter at him, save Balder, who kept his eyes as much as

possible away from the crooked, ugly, mighty, unlaugh-
ing God. Loki was very nearly smiling. . . .

' Loki,' said Har, ' turned away from this game.'

' When his back was turned,' said Gangler, ' he smiled,
I am sure, as Erne the fool did once when I was a boy;
and that night the old king had a dream and awoke
mad, and never said any wise thing again except that
Erne ought to be king.'

' I was saying,' said Har, ' that Loki turned away from
this game. He went away to change himself into the
likeness of a woman. When he had done so he came
to Frigga's mansion and said to her : " They are all
hewing and hurling at Balder." She laughed and said :

' " Yes, I know. No weapon can hurt Balder. All
things of wood and metal have sworn it."

' " Has every single thing made this promise ? "
asked the pretended woman.

' " Yes, everything."

' " You were wise."

' " He is my dearest child. I could not rest until all
had sworn "—then she laughed—" all except that little
bush of mistletoe growing in the poplar-tree on the east
side of Valhalla."

' Loki also laughed. Then he went quickly away
and changed into his own shape. He trimmed a piece
of the mistletoe into a dart, and went with it to the
place where the Gods were again at the same sport with
Balder. Only one was not playing, and that was Hod
the Blind.

' " Why are you not playing, Hod ? " asked Loki.

' " Because I am blind, and I have nothing to throw."

' " They are all too busy to look after you," said
Loki, handing him the mistletoe. " Take this dart, then,
and pay honour to Balder."

' Hod took the dart and turned as Loki directed him, until he was facing Balder ; then he threw.

' A laugh went up at the sight of the blind God throwing his little dart. Some of them continued to laugh even when the dart entered Balder's eye. Then the beautiful God fell to the ground. At first all were silent in astonishment, because he lay still : only Hod was laughing. It was now that Odin came up. He looked at Balder and at Hod, and he knew well what had happened. Balder was dead. All burst into loud lamentations, except Odin, who stood silent over the body, and Loki, who crept away.

' At length Odin spoke :

' " Weep no more, Gods and companions. Balder was doomed, and he is dead. We also are doomed, and we are yet alive : nothing remains for us but to bury him like a God, and to live on the life of Gods until we must die. Eat and drink to-night, and to-morrow build the funeral pile on Balder's ship, and send it out with fire into the sea." Then Odin left them, and they sat down in silence and took their cups from the hands of the Valkyries. Hod alone would not join the feast. He made his way sadly to Frigga's palace, Fensaler, and told his story. She, who knew everything, knew what had happened. She did not blame the blind thrower, but she said something might yet be done. If one would take Sleipnir, Odin's horse, and ride to Hell, he might persuade its queen to let Balder return. Hod was willing to go, and yet he was helpless, as Frigga knew. She bade him return to Asgard and reveal the plan to the first one whom he should meet. When he returned the feast had broken up, and the Gods had carried Balder to his own palace of Breidablik. But Hod met one of them, the swiftest of all the Gods, named Hermod.

He told Hermod what Frigga had said, and bade him saddle Sleipnir. He himself went home, fixed his sword upright in the floor, and fell on it and died.

'Early in the morning the Gods, led by Frey on his boar with the golden tusks, carried Balder's body down to his ship, which stood dry upon the shore. But they could not launch the ship. So they sent to Giantland for the Giantess Hyrrokin to help them. She came swiftly riding on her wolf, which she guided with a bridle of twisted snakes. When she had alighted, the warriors who took charge of her steed had to throw it to the ground before he would stay still. With one touch Hyrrokin sent the ship sliding over the shingle into the sea, but so rapidly that the keel caught fire. This infuriated Thor; he seized his hammer, and could hardly be prevented from breaking the skull of the Giantess. The Gods carried down pine-trees and made a pile in the middle of the ship, and on it they laid the body. This sight broke the heart of Nanna, Balder's wife, and her body was laid beside his. All the Gods were on the shore, standing gloomy and tall like a long grove of trees. The ravens were perched on Odin's shoulder. The Giants stood a little apart. The Dwarfs were gathered in a multitude among the rocks at the foot of the sea-cliffs, but a few of them went in and out among the Gods like starlings among sheep. All mourned for Balder in silence, until the flames began to flap higher and wider than the sails had ever been; and as if driven along by the flames instead of sails, the ship rolled out into the sea. The wind was blowing strong from the land, but had there been no wind the breath of all that assembly mourning for Balder and crying farewell to him would have been strong enough to waft the ship. Their cries frightened all the sea-birds from their nests in the

cliffs. The birds seemed to be silent, so loud was the
lamentation, until the moment when the flames far
away sank down into the sea like a bird settling in its
nest. Not a sound was heard after that except the
seagulls. The Dwarfs retired into the rocks. The
Giants trooped up over the cliff. The Gods in twos and
threes, and some solitary, turned away last.

'At Asgard, many days afterwards, Hermod appeared.
For nine days and nights he had been journeying in dark
glens, where, he said, the blind Hod could have found
a way as well as he. He was long among those mountains which Niord, the father of Freya, loathed, though
he was there only nine nights. "The howl of the
wolves," he said, "seemed evil to me after the song of
the swans." At last Hermod came to the river Gioll,
on this side of Hell. A bridge of gold spanned the river,
but at the other side the maiden Modgunn asked him
his name and race. She said that five companies of
dead men had ridden over the bridge on the day before,
and had not shaken it so much as he. He was no dead
man. What right had he to cross into Hell? He told
her that he was seeking Balder in Hell, and asked had
she seen him pass. She said that Balder had crossed,
and that Hermod must go north to reach Hell. He went
on with his journey until he halted before the gates.
There he alighted, tightened his saddle-girths, mounted,
and struck both spurs into Sleipnir and leaped over.
Balder was sitting on a throne in Hell, and Hermod
sat talking with him all night. In the morning he
begged the queen to let Balder come back with him.
He told her that all Gods and men and all created
things were sorrowing for Balder. She answered that
if all of them desired Balder's return he should go,
but if any one spoke against him, or refused to mourn,

he must stay. Hermod rose to take back the message, bringing with him a ring for Odin from Balder, and a linen mantle for Frigga from Nanna. These presents he now gave to Odin and Frigga.

'The Gods sent messengers all over the world, bidding all things to weep, in order that Balder might be rescued from Hell. Even to the stones and grasses, all things obeyed, as they would have obeyed the command of Spring or Winter. The messengers came back rejoicing in spite of their tears. But as they were nearing Asgard they met an old hag at the opening of a cave. They begged her also to weep. She answered that she had done with weeping. Who was Balder, that she should weep for him, alive or dead? She had no tears left. "Let the Queen of Hell keep what she has : it is better so." Some thought that this hag was Loki, but nevertheless Balder remained in Hell.'

After hearing the story of Balder, Gangler exclaimed :

'How can the Gods allow such an evil one as Loki to live? Did they not punish him for these crimes? What was Thor's hammer doing? Why did they not put Loki on the funeral pile?'

'Softly, softly,' said Thridi; 'in the end Loki was paid his wages. You do not understand that he was just as much a God as any of the others. He could not be wiped out by a stroke of the sword, although he did nothing but what was painful or hateful to men as well as Gods. He was the son of a Giant.'

'Being only the son of a Giant,' said Gangler, 'why did they let him continue his life of crime and mischief?'

'Well, there it is. He did continue,' answered Har. 'He has not his equal for cunning and treachery, and in his way he is very mighty. He has led the Gods into danger, and has led them out again. His children are mighty, especially those whose mother was the Giantess Angurbodi. The wolf Fenrir, the serpent Jormungand, and Hela the Queen of Hell, are his children by this wife. When the Gods heard of this family growing up in Giantland they were alarmed; they inquired into the future, and learnt that these children were to be an evil and busy race. Odin thought it best to send one of the Gods to fetch the children. They came. Odin looked at them and they at him, but they paid one another no compliments, nor indeed spoke words of any kind. Odin threw the serpent into the ocean which surrounds Midgard like a ring; but it did not die though it stayed in the water; its tail grew in one direction, its head in another, so that now it has completely encircled Midgard and holds its tail in its mouth.

Hela was cast into Niflheim. There she became Queen of Hell, and every one, man or God, who dies in any way except in battle, goes to Niflheim and becomes her subject. Her palace is very high, and the gates of it very strong. Her hall is called Misery. Her table is Hunger; her knife, Starvation; her man, Delay; her maid, Sloth; her threshold, Ruin; her bed, Care; and the curtains and tapestry of her room are Burning Anguish. She cannot disguise herself. Though she does not speak, men know what is in her mind. She has a mirk face, grim and unchanging.

Hela's brother, Fenrir the wolf, remained with the Gods. From the first he snapped at the hand that fed him. Only Tyr at last would go near him. He thrived upon his food, whatever it was, and he grew to an enormous size and did not stop growing. The Gods were warned that Fenrir would one day be the death of them. They therefore made up their minds to

appear to be his masters until the day appointed. They
had an iron fetter forged for him, and as they asked him
to show how strong he was he allowed himself to be
bound with the fetter. He burst the fetter with ease,
and they tried to pretend not to be surprised. They
made another fetter that was far stronger, and persuaded
him to put it on by saying that there would be no
doubt about his strength if he could break this ; as to
the other one, it was a jest, and they were sorry for
making a fool of him. As the wolf could not speak, he
said nothing, but allowed himself to be fettered. When
he was bound he shook himself, took a deep breath,
and threw himself on the ground, rolling over and over.
Thus he broke the second fetter.

' The Gods could not conceal their despair. But Odin
sent a messenger into the country of the Dark Elves,
asking the Dwarfs to make a fetter to bind Fenrir. The
Dwarfs made it smooth and soft as silk. For in making
it they used the beards of women, the roots of stones, the
breath of fish, and the sound of a cat's foot. The Gods
were pleased with it, not so much because of its strength,
which they had not tested, but because it was the work
of the Dwarfs. They showed Fenrir this cord and begged
him to try his strength on it, and to prove that it was
stronger than it seemed they each took it in turn and
failed to break it. " No one can do it except Fenrir,"
they said. Fenrir appeared to be unwilling. He looked
scornfully at the cord, as much as to say that he would
get no glory by breaking such a slender bond. On the
other hand, if its thickness gave no idea of its strength
it would be wise to keep out of it. The Gods began to be
puffed up with pride at the respect which Fenrir showed
for the Dwarfs' cord. They said to one another,
" Evidently he is afraid of it, and if he is too weak to

break it we need not be afraid of him, but can safely
set him free at once." Fenrir could not refuse; but
neither could they force him to accept. He made one
condition, that he should hold the hand of one of
the Gods in his mouth as a pledge. Tyr was the only
one who offered his hand. He put it instantly between
Fenrir's jaws. Then the Gods fastened the cord.
Fenrir stretched and strained and rolled, but without
loosening or breaking the cord. The Gods roared with
laughter, all except Tyr, whose hand was bitten off. They
made haste now to fasten the wolf to a rock that was
sunk deep in the earth. He could not break loose,
yet he did not cease trying to do so, and the sight of
his mighty but helpless jaws opening and shutting
frightened and at last irritated the Gods. So one of
them thrust a sword into his mouth to make him shut
it. The wolf now began to howl, and a river of foam
ran out of his mouth. The river will run, and Fenrir
will howl, until Ragnarok.'

'Oh, why did the Gods leave the wolf alive?' asked
Gangler.

'Because,' said Har, 'there is a rule that the place
where Fenrir is bound should not be stained with blood.'

'I see,' said Gangler.

V

LOKI; AND THE HORSE AND THE SHIP

GANGLER was wondering why Loki never drove any of the Gods mad, as Erne the Fool drove the king mad when he was a boy; and why they never thought of putting him up in the chief place among them instead of Odin.

' I wonder,' he said, ' that Loki is not the first of the Gods instead of Odin, since he is the father of Fenrir.'

' No,' said Har, ' that is not likely to happen yet, for Loki is now the least important of all the Gods.

' One day the Gods and Goddesses, all except Thor and Loki, were feasting at the hall of Eager, the Sea God. It was the first time they had laughed as of old since Balder's death; Loki had not reappeared, and there was nothing to spoil the feast. That lying, deceitful God had been slinking about, not in shame but fear. Now, however, he was slinking back. He heard Odin's thundering laughter, and he said to himself: "They have forgotten Balder. They will forgive me as easily." But first he asked the cook what the Gods were talking about as they drank. "They are talking of their swords and spears, and the deeds they have done," said the cook, " but no one has a good word to say of you, Loki." At this he vowed that he would put poison into the Gods' drink, but he entered the hall smiling.'

Gangler muttered : ' I do not believe he was really smiling, any more than Erne when his lips curled and twitched.'

Har was not to be disturbed, and went on with his tale.

' " I am thirsty after a long journey," said Loki, " and I beg for one draught of your mead."

' No one answered.

' " Why do ye sit silent and sulky ? Give me a seat or drive me away."

' Bragi answered, saying :

' " The Gods will never give thee a seat at any joyous feast."

' Loki turned to Odin :

' " Dost thou remember how we two long ago blended blood together ? We swore never to drink except together."

' Odin knew the knavery of Loki, and did not smile ; neither was his heart moved ; yet he said :

' " Give him a place. That is better than hearing his nasty tongue."

' Loki sat down and drank a health to Odin and the other Gods, all except Bragi. To quiet him, Bragi promised him a steed, a sword, and many rings, but in vain. Loki taunted him that he was a coward, and never had horse or arm-rings. Bragi grew angry and threatening : Loki kept on quietly taunting, and when Iduna, Bragi's wife, begged her husband to let him go on and not answer him, he insulted her also. Others now spoke, trying to heal the strife either by threats or by mild words ; but Loki had insults for all of them, and was so much quicker and quieter of speech, and kept in his seat so modestly, that they knew not what to do. Odin turned on him and said :

' " Loki, thou art drunk and foolish."

But Loki had the last word. So he did with Frigga, when she begged Loki not to talk before the warriors about what Odin and the other Gods had done in their young days. Nor had Freya any more success. When-

ever any God or Goddess mentioned something shameful
in Loki's history to try to silence him with shame, he invented something far worse about his accuser, who either
could not or would not go on answering such a scullion.
Heimdal said to him: " Thou art drunk, Loki, and out of
thy wits. Too much drinking makes men babble without
meaning." " Shut thy mouth, Heimdal. What dost
thou know about anything, with thy dull life, always
standing by the bridge with a wet back as the Gods'
watchman ? " Big, simple old Heimdal gaped in
astonishment. Thor's wife, Sif, then handed Loki
a goblet to quiet him, saying :

' " Now hail to thee, Loki, and take this foaming cup
of old mead, and let at least one of the Gods go without
an insult."

' But he drank the mead, and insulted her while his
lips were wet with it. No answer came, and what with
the mead and the fatigue of listening to such fools as the
Gods, he was dozing off to sleep, still muttering vile insults
half to himself, and laughing at them. As his eyes
were half shut he did not see Thor enter, but he had
no need of his quick ears to hear Thor speak.

' " Be quiet, cur," said Thor, " or my hammer shall
stop thy mouth and thy life at the same time."

' Loki started, but did not change his manner, except
that he took up the empty goblet and looked into it,
wishing he could drink. Then he said :

' " Ha ! here is Thor, talking big as usual. Why talk
so big ? Thou wilt not be so bold when it comes to
fighting the wolf who is to swallow up Odin himself."

' " Peace, Loki," said Thor, " or I will fling thee out,
and then break every bone in thy body."

' " I mean to have a long life," said Loki, " in spite
of that hammer, which is more suitable for felling an ox,

or some one like Heimdal, or Odin, the father of us all, than for breaking my small bones."

' " Oh, br-r-r," said Thor in fury, unable to find a word to stop his mouth with ; and Loki, who knew perfectly well what he meant, got up and went away quietly, but nevertheless very swiftly. Once only he turned, to whisper to Eager, his host :

' " This will be thy last banquet, Eager. The flame shall lick up everything here, and burn thy back also." '

'He got off easily enough,' said Gangler, ' and every one else got off worse.'

' That was not the end,' said Jafnhar. ' When he was outside the hall he ran, and did not stop until he reached the mountains. There he made himself a house on a summit, with four doors, so that he could see on every side. For fear of the Gods, he never went out in his proper shape, but would spend his time at the foot of a waterfall in the likeness of a salmon, and in one shape or another he often heard the plans of the Gods for catching him. One day he was sitting alone with some flax and yarn, and he invented net-making such as fishermen afterwards used. But Odin, sitting high up, on Lidskialf, spied him out in his house, and the Gods set out against him. Loki was not to be surprised. He threw his net into the fire and ran to the waterfall, where he hid himself. The Gods found his dwelling empty, but one of them saw the burnt yet unbroken net lying like the ghost of a net in the ashes. They saw at once what it could be used for ; they made another on this model, and with it went down to fish for the Loki salmon. Thor held one end of the net and the rest held the other, and so they dragged it from end to end of the pool under the waterfall. Loki, however, lay pressed down between two stones, and the net passed over him.

They dragged the pool a second time, weighting the net
so that it scraped up stones and all. But Loki leapt
over the net and swam down the stream. The Gods
followed after him, Thor alone running in mid-stream
behind the net, in case he should turn back; and so he
did, with a great leap which ended in Thor's hand.
Thor had him by the tail, and as salmon's tails were
thicker then and less slippery than they are now, Loki did
not escape. He now changed his form, but got no more
pity as a God than as a salmon. The Gods dragged him
to a cave, and placed in it three spiky rocks in a row,
and bound Loki face upwards on their points. One of
them hung up a serpent to the roof of the cave above him,
so that its venom should drip on to his face. But Loki's
wife would not allow him to suffer in this manner.
She stood—and she still stands—beside him, catching the
drops in a cup. When the cup is full she empties away
the venom, and while she is doing so one drop always falls
on Loki, which makes him howl and twist in spite of the
pointed rocks. It is this twisting of Loki down in the
cave that causes what men call earthquakes. There
he will lie until Ragnarok, after which there will be no
more earthquakes.'

' And, I hope, no more Loki,' said Gangler.

' Who shall say ? ' said Har. ' All we know is that at
present Odin is the greatest of Gods, as the ash Yggdrasil
is the greatest of trees; Skidbladnir the greatest of
ships, Sleipnir of steeds, Bifrost of bridges, Bragi of
bards, Habrok of hawks, and Garm of hounds.'

' Thou hast mentioned Sleipnir more than once,' said
Gangler. ' What is there to say about him ? '

' Thou seemest to be entirely ignorant in this matter
of Sleipnir, but thou wilt find it worth while to listen to
what I shall say of it.

' Once, when the Gods were building their homes here
and there, a Giant workman came and offered himself
for the work. He undertook to build a palace so strong
that the Giants could not break into it, even if they
should ever get over into Midgard. The price to be
paid was the Goddess Freya, the sun, and the moon.
The Gods thought it over and decided that they would
pay the price, on these conditions : that he would finish
the work without any one's help, and all in one winter;
if anything remained to be done on the first day of
summer the workman would have to go without his
price. He, on his part, was willing to accept these conditions : only, he asked to be allowed to make use of his
horse, Svadilfari. This, on the advice of Loki, was
granted.

' He was to begin his work on the first day of winter,
and on the night before his horse was drawing stone for
the building. When morning dawned the Gods came to
look on, and they wondered very much at the size of the
stones, for if hollowed out any one of them would have
made a house for a man. They saw that the horse was
doing the main part of the work. However, they had
sworn oaths in the presence of witnesses undertaking
to pay this man his price, and to let him have the
help of a horse. He had insisted on such oaths as a
Giant expects before trusting himself among the Gods.

' Some time before winter's end the palace was almost
ready. It was huge, and as firm as the earth itself.
It was too high to be scaled by anything but birds
or clouds. There were three days still to come before
summer when only the gateway remained to be done.
The Gods now began to think seriously about their
bargain. When they made it they did not really think
that the man could do the work, or that, if he did, they

would really have to give him Freya, the sun, and the
moon. They now tried to recall who it was that first
overcame their objection to this monstrous price, to
send Freya away and to take down the sun and moon
out of the sky. They agreed that it was Loki. He had
done many evil and mischievous deeds ; only he could
have suggested this ; and therefore he should be put
to death, unless he could think of some way of getting
out of this bargain. In fact they laid hands on him,
and threatened him with a good will until he made
a promise to outwit the workman.

'That night, as the builder and his horse went out
to fetch stone, a mare ran out from the forest which
came on all sides to the edge of the quarry. She neighed
and ran back again. Svadilfari also neighed. He forgot
that he was going to haul stone, and started to run. When
he came to a block, he leapt over it and left the wagon
behind. Svadilfari ran after the mare, and the builder
after Svadilfari. He ran all night, but lost his horse.
His task was far beyond the strength of any man.
But, it seems, he was not a man, but a Giant, and he
now changed himself back into his true Giant shape and
set to work. When the Gods saw that he was a Mountain
Giant, they remembered their oaths only in order to break
them. They called for Thor to pay the Giant his wages.
This he did without waiting until the appointed day.
He brought not Freya, not the sun, and not the moon,
but only his own hammer. With this he struck the
Giant a blow that broke his skull, so that he could not
have taken away his wages even had they been offered
to him as well as what he had already received.'

'But what of Sleipnir ? '

'Sleipnir was born some time afterwards. He was
the son of Svadilfari. He was a grey and had eight

legs, and he became the swiftest and strongest of all the horses that ever carried Gods or men. He is Odin's horse. As you know, he carried Odin to Giantland and Hermod to Hell.'

' Is there any story like this about Skidbladnir, the best of ships ? ' said Gangler. ' Is it the largest or is it the best ? '

' It is the best. I did not say the largest,' said Har, ' Naglfar is a larger ship, the ship of Hell which will sail at the end, after Ragnarok. The Dwarfs built Skidbladnir as a present for Freya. They built her of the nails of dead men, and they repair her with the same material. She will hold all the Gods, with their weapons and stores of war. When her sails are hoisted, a breeze springs up and carries her swift and safe to whatever place the Gods choose. She is made of thousands of little pieces, fitted together with so much cleverness that when she is not wanted Freya can fold her up and keep her in her pocket.'

' I should like to have seen the Dwarfs building Skidbladnir. But are there any sea-dwarfs ? I thought the Dwarfs belonged to the mountains and the bowels of the earth.'

' So they do.'

' Then what do they know about the sea ?'

' Ask the Dwarfs. They know enough to have made the ship Skidbladnir, which is the best of all ships, and the best quality of it is that a God is as safe on it as on the land. For the Dwarfs were land-dwarfs. If it had been made by creatures of the sea, perhaps it would have been as dangerous as the sea.'

' Oh ! ' said Gangler.

VI

THOR

GANGLER was still thinking of Sleipnir and his eight legs. He could not imagine a horse with eight legs at first, until he remembered seeing one himself. It was galloping along the edge of a dense wood in the moonlight, and his shadow was clear beside him, so that there were eight legs galloping together.

'Did Sleipnir ever race to show that he was the best of horses?' he asked.

'Once Odin was riding Sleipnir towards Giantland, and the Giant Rungnir looked out of his door. . . .'

It was very odd, but those words, ' the Giant Rungnir looked out of his door,' painted a picture of house and Giant on Gangler's brain in less than a second. It was a house like the side of a woody hill, and the door was like a huge chalk-pit cut in the hill, and the Giant was stooping to look out, as if he were so tall that when he stood up his head reached to the inside of the hill-top or house. Rungnir was one of the red-haired Giants, and his beard glistened as if the inside of his house were damp with cookery.

'And as Rungnir looked out he said to himself, " Who can that be with the helmet of gold riding over sky and sea? He has a wonderful good horse." Odin heard him and said : " I would bet my head there is not a horse in Giantland equal to Sleipnir." " Tut ! " said Rungnir, " it is a good enough horse, but my Goldmane is better."

' Odin answered :

' " Your Goldmane would go faster if Sleipnir were carrying him than if he ran with his own four feet."

' Rungnir was angry. He at once leapt up on Goldmane and galloped after Odin. But he could only just see Odin at last, disappearing through Asgard gates. There could be no doubt that Sleipnir was the better horse, and Odin said : " You should have let him carry Goldmane if you wanted to keep up with him." Rungnir entered after him : in fact he rode right into the hall where the Gods were drinking, and called out for drink. They brought him mead in the bowl that Thor used to drink from, and he emptied it again and again. He lolled about in his seat, talking big and beastly. He said he could take up Valhalla and carry it to Giantland, and he could slay all the Gods except Freya and Sif, whom he would take away for wives. Freya was the only one who dared to carry drink to him now. He boasted that he would drink up all the Gods' ale.

' The Gods got tired of his boasting. Then Thor came in with his hammer, and asked :

' " How comes it that dogs of Giants drink here? Why should Freya carry drink to the fellow ?'

' Rungnir said :

' " Odin invited me."

' " Well," said Thor, " you can stay, but you shall be sorry for it."

' " Much glory you may get, Thor ! " said Rungnir, " from a foe without weapons. But if I had my shield and my hone I should like nothing better than a fight."

' " Get you gone, then, to Giantland," said Thor, " and we will fight it out there."

' The Giants were proud of Rungnir for his journey to Asgard, but they were also anxious as to the battle.

Rungnir was the mightiest of the Giants, and if he
should fall there was no knowing what Thor might do
when swollen with pride of victory. They made a Giant
out of clay, bigger even than Rungnir, to stand by his
side and strike Thor with fear. This Giant of clay was
called Muck-calf, and in spite of his size he was afraid
of Thor. With Thor came his servant Thialfi, and Thialfi
met Muck-calf, while Thor went up against Rungnir. The
God began the battle by hurling his hammer, but the
Giant cast his hone almost at the same time. The hone
broke in two against the hammer, and one half crashed
into Thor's head, so that he fell to the earth. The hammer found its way to Rungnir's head and broke into
it. The Giant fell, but with one of his feet over the
neck of the prostrate Thor: it stiffened with death,
and Thialfi, who had easily upset the Muck-calf, could not
move it; and there lay Thor helpless in the caress of that
enormous foot. He was released at last by his own son,
Magni, whose mother was a Giantess. Magni had the
horse Goldmane as his reward from Thor, though Odin
was angry that the son of a Giantess should have it.
The half of the Giant's hone was still fast in Thor's head
when he came home. A sibyl named Groa, the wife
of Orion the Brave, tried to get it out by chanting spell
songs. Thor believed that it was loosening, and he felt
very grateful to Groa. So in his gratitude he told her
a piece of news. He had been travelling over Sleet Bay
from the North, and took Orion with him in his basket.
But one of Orion's toes had been sticking out, and so
got frozen. Thor had taken this useless frostbitten toe
and cast it up into the heavens, and made the star with it
which is called Orion's toe. Orion was limping slightly,
but he would be home very soon, said Thor. Groa was
excited by this news; she was sorry about the toe,

proud about the star, and glad about her husband's return ; and off she went without finishing her spells. Therefore the hone is still in Thor's head.'

' Thor is in every story,' said Gangler.

' He is the mightiest of the Gods,' said Har, and as he uttered the words his voice shook the roof of shields, and roused the other two kings to say also in voices like the sea : ' Thor is the mightiest of the Gods.' And Gangler muttered as if he were a child repeating a lesson : ' Thor is the mightiest of the Gods.' It seemed to him that Thor must be such a one as Jafnhar, the king who was now sitting before him in a throne of gold. He had been looking at Jafnhar and thinking of him not seated on a throne, but speaking and walking about. For without his throne Jafnhar was like a man whom Gangler remembered—a bearded red-faced captain coming home from war. Gangler had seen the man once only for a moment, with a newly emptied mead-horn in his hand, and his head thrown back, laughing among his companions by a roadside in the sun. He never heard the man speak or saw him do anything, yet he fancied that this man could have ruled the world. Still more did he think so now, seeing the image of this man seated on a throne before him, saying in his great voice : ' Thor is the mightiest of the Gods.' The man laughing in the sun had perhaps been Thor himself. But Har continued :

' Thor is perhaps what Odin was when he was young, and what he might still have been had he not become so wise and benevolent as he is. But Thor also is wise in his way. His palace is Bilstirnir, the largest of all houses. He rides in a chariot drawn by two goats. He has three famous possessions. First is his hammer, called Miolnir. It is famous chiefly among the Frost Giants and Mountain Giants, because he has broken many of their skulls with it—I mean the skulls of their friends and relations, for those whose skulls are broken make the hammer famous indeed, but are not alive to observe its fame. Thor has also a belt that is above all others; when he puts it on his strength is twice what it was before. The third possession is a pair of iron gauntlets; these he has to wear when he is using his hammer, Miolnir.'

' Supposing,' said Gangler, ' supposing some one stole Miolnir and the gauntlets as well. Would they be of any use to any one but Thor? '

' It has never been tried,' answered Har, ' but once the hammer was stolen. Thor woke up, and saw instantly that the hammer had gone in the night. He shook his beard and tossed his locks in anger. The hammer was nowhere to be seen. " Loki," said Thor, " I have lost my hammer."

' They went together to Freya's bower, and Thor asked her to lend him her feather-dress to help him find his hammer. She gladly lent it. Loki put it on, and away he flew out of Asgard towards Giantland. Thrym, the lord of the Giants, was sitting on a mound plaiting golden leashes for his greyhounds, when he looked up and saw Loki.

' " What news is there of the Gods? " he asked, " how are the Elves? Why hast thou come alone, Loki? "

' " It goes ill with the Gods," he answered. " Is it thou, Thrym, that hast hidden the Thunderer's hammer? "

' " It is, Loki. I have hidden Miolnir eight miles under ground. No man shall ever get it back unless he brings me Freya as a wife."

' Loki made no answer, but flew off to Asgard. Thor

spied him while he was still high in air, and asked him to give his news immediately.

' " I have good news," said Loki. " I know where the hammer is—with the Giant lord, Thrym. But it cannot be recovered unless Freya is given to him as wife.'

' Thor went straight to Freya, and bade her make ready to go to Giantland. She refused, and snapped her necklace in her fury. She could not speak for some time, and when she did she only said : " I should be the man-maddest of women to drive with thee to Giantland." So the Gods took counsel together as to how to recover Miolnir.

' " I have a plan," said Heimdal. " Let us dress up Thor like Freya. Let him put on her bride's veil and her hood, put her necklace on his neck, let her keys hang down from his girdle rattling, and wear her brooches on his breast."

' " I am not going to be dressed up like a woman," blurted Thor.

' " If you don't," said Loki, " you will not get your hammer, and the Giants will take up their abode in Asgard."

' So Thor let them dress him up, and he was very glad to have the veil put on first to hide his shame. " I will be the bridesmaid," said Loki. The goats were fetched and harnessed to Thor's chariot. As they raged along the rocks were torn up and the earth blazed in flame.

' Thrym was glad at the sight. " Stand up," he said, " stand up, my Giants all, and make ready the benches. They are bringing me a wife from Asgard, Freya, the daughter of Niord. I had golden-horned cows and black unspotted oxen, I had treasures and jewels—I had these already. But now I have Freya."

' There was a great gathering of Giants feasting and

drinking ale in the evening at the bridal of Thrym. The
false Freya ate a whole ox, eight salmon, and all the
dainties that had been cooked for the ladies. She also
drank three casks of mead.

' Said Thrym :

' " Was ever a bride so ravenous before ? I have never
seen one take such mouthfuls or drink such draughts."

' The bridesmaid Loki had an answer ready :

' " Freya has not eaten for eight days, no ! not once
during our journey, so eager was she to be in Giantland."

' Thrym grew vain as well as glad. He had been a
little shy of his bride, but now he thought to give her
a kiss. He bent down under the veil to do so ; then
started back the whole length of the hall. " Why," he
asked, " are Freya's eyes so terrible ?   It is as if flames
were darting from them."

' " That is very natural," said Loki. " She has not
slept for eight nights, so eager was she to be in Giantland."

' The Giant's aged mother came in to beg of Freya.
" Give me the red-gold rings from thine arm," she said,
" if thou wouldst win my love and my heart."

' The bride took no notice ; neither did the Giant,
but called out for the hammer to be brought to make
the bargain complete. " Lay Miolnir in the maid's lap,"
he shouted.

' Thor was as glad as any bride when the hammer was
laid in his lap. His heart laughed in his breast, and his
eyes and teeth flashed through the veil, as he grasped
the hammer. " Now thou shalt have the hammer back
again, my love," said Thor, and it sank deep into the
Giant's skull. His blows were all the heavier because the
veil made him angry with shame. He smote the whole
company of Giants before he took off his veil and

became a God again. He was very near striking Loki
for putting him to this humiliation, although the result
of it was that Miolnir was in his hand.'

'Tell me,' said Gangler, 'one of the adventures that
Thor was not ashamed of.'

'There are many of them,' said Har, 'in fact there is
only one other that he is ashamed of, and that is the
adventure with the ferryman.

'He was travelling alone one day on foot, when he
came to a river where there was a ferry, but the ferry-boat
was on the other side and the ferryman was standing in
it, looking over at Thor but not showing any sign of
crossing.

'"Hi!" shouted Thor, pretty loudly. There was no
answer.

'"Hi!" he shouted again, so loud that all the fish
in the river gave a start. But the ferryman neither
answered nor moved. Thor stood waiting some little
time without repeating his call, because he felt quite
certain that the man had heard. Then he put one hand
on each side of his mouth and yelled. He paused an
instant to see whether the ferryman would speak, and
then yelled and hallooed his loudest, as if it were a game.
When he could shout no longer he stopped. The ferryman said quietly :

'"Hullo!"

'"Are you deaf?" asked Thor.

'"No, but likely to become so if you stay there,"
said the ferryman.

'"What lad are you? You look starved."

'"What churl are you?"

'"Ferry me over the water, and I will give thee
plenty of food to-morrow. I have a basket on my back ;
there was never better meat ; but as I dined on herring

and goat-venison before I started, I do not want it myself."

' " An early meal, fellow. But you fed better than you dressed, and I dare say you will have to beg your next meal as you did your clothes, by the look of them."

' " Come, bring the boat over. Who owns her ? "

' " His name is Hildwolf, and he told me to keep her here. He is the shrewd farmer who lives at Radsey Sound. He told me not to ferry over any poachers or horse-thieves or the likes of you, but only good men and such as I knew well. Tell me who you are, if you wish to cross."

' " I am Odin's son, Magni's father, the Strong One of the Gods. It is with Thor you are speaking. Now what is your name ? "

' " Hoarbeard. I never hide my name."

' " Why should you, unless you are an outlaw whom all men can insult."

' " Even if I were, I should have no fear of such as you."

' " It is not a task I like, to wade through the river to get at you. If I did cross I should pay you well for your mockery."

' " Well, here I am, waiting for you. You won't come ? I know you, Thor, a big strong fellow, with no heart. They talk far too much about you. Do you remember when you were hid in a glove, in deadly fear lest you should sneeze and betray yourself ? "

' " You are the one with no heart, Hoarbeard, talking like this with a river between you and me. I should be the death of you if I could reach you. But where did you learn to answer so sharply, Hoarbeard ? "

' " The old Giantesses who live in the burial-mounds were my teachers."

' " Well, your sharpness will do you no good if I get
at you."

' " But you won't, Thor. You had better go back
and look after your wife. Really, I never dreamed that
a ferryman could stop the mighty Thor."

' " Now come. Let us give up shouting. Just pull the
boat over for me."

' " Not I ! "

' " Then tell me another way."

' " You go on for two hours on that road, and then turn
to the left at the stone and keep on till you come to
Werland. There you will find your mother, and she will
put you on the main road for Odin's country."

' " Shall I get there to-day ? "

' " If you walk hard you will get there at sunrise or
thereabouts."

' " And now I will leave you, as you have nothing but
mocking for me. But I will pay you back if we meet
again."

' " Go, then, and bad luck to you."

' Was that ferryman a God of some sort in disguise ? '
asked Gangler.

' No ! ' said Har, ' but he was a ferryman, and he was
on the other side of the water, which was deep.'

VII

THOR'S DEFEAT

' TELL me,' said Gangler, ' was Thor ever actually
beaten either by enchantment or by sheer force ? '

' Few would care to say so,' answered Har, ' and yet
it is certain that he has often been hard pressed. Had
he been altogether worsted no one would mention it,
because all are bound to believe that Thor is irresistible.'

' Then apparently I have asked you a question which
you either will not or cannot answer ? '

' There are rumours,' said Jafnhar, ' but they are not
to be believed. Nevertheless, there is one sitting here
who can tell thee, and he speaks the truth.'

' I shall gladly listen and satisfy myself whether you
can or cannot answer my question, which was, Did
any one ever beat Thor by enchantment or by sheer
force ? '

Thridi now spoke :

' Thy curiosity is natural, but it will be well for thee
to be silent about what thou shalt hear.

' One day Thor set out with Loki upon a journey
in his chariot drawn by two goats. At nightfall they
stopped and lodged at a peasant's cottage, and for
supper Thor killed the goats, skinned them, and put
them in the pot. When the meat was ready, the two
Gods sat down and invited the peasant and his family
to share their supper. When they had finished eating,
Thor bade them throw all the bones into the goats' skins
which had been spread out near the fireplace, but the

peasant's son, whose name was Thialfi, had lingered over the meal and cracked one of the shank-bones to get at the marrow.

'Thor was up early. The first thing he did was to go over to the skins and bones of the two goats and bless them, lifting up his hammer as he did so. Instantly the living forms of two goats took the place of the torn skins and the bare bones. There was one difference : one of the goats now limped on one of its hind legs. " One of you," said Thor to the peasants, " must have been careless. At least you have broken a bone. See how the poor thing is limping." Thor was angry, knitting his brows and clenching his hand upon his hammer so that his knuckles were white as milk. The peasants were in deadly fear, and the old man said : " Tell us, we beg of you, what we can do to make up for our offence. If we had had any idea what you were going to do with the old bones we should have been wiser and carefuller. Forgive us our folly and disobedience." Thor's anger was over at once when he saw how it had frightened these good people. He spoke kindly to them, but took away with him the boy Thialfi and the girl Roska to serve him, and they do so to this day. He left the goats behind at the cottage, and went on with Loki and his servants.

'They were travelling eastward on the road to Giant-land, and came after many miles to the shores of a great sea. This they crossed and entered a strange country. They had not gone far when they saw before them an immense forest. Here they wandered all day until it was dark. They stopped for the night in a vast hall open at one end, which they found in the midst of the forest. At about midnight they were disturbed in their sleep by an earthquake, which made the floor move as if it had been water. Thor got up, and called to the others to look with him for a place of safety. They found another room leading out of the hall, and the other three crept into the farthest corner of it. Thor stood at the entrance with his hammer ready in case they were attacked. But nothing happened, except that all through the night something seemed to be groaning horribly close by. At dawn Thor discovered that this was really the snoring of a Giant who lay outside and was still asleep. The God put on his belt to increase his strength, and waited. Presently the Giant awoke, turned sleepily over on to his back looking at Thor, and then rose upright to an enormous height. He did this so rapidly that Thor was as much astonished at it as the peasants were at the bones turning into goats. Doubtless it was his lying down in the night that produced the earthquake. Thor did nothing but ask the Giant his name.

' " Skrymir," said the Giant. " I need not ask your name, for I see that you are the God Thor. But what have you been doing with my glove ? " As he said this he picked up his glove, which, as was now quite plain, was really what they had supposed to be a hall, while the room which they entered after the earthquake was the thumb of the glove. This was the time when Thor hid in a glove, as the ferryman Hoarbeard reminded him. Skrymir was as amiable as a mountain. He asked if they would care for his company, and when Thor agreed he opened his wallet and had his breakfast. Thor and Loki and their servants also breakfasted, and when they had done so Skrymir said that they had better put all their provisions together, and this they did; the Giant put everything into his wallet, and carried it on his back all day. He walked on in front, and his strides were very

long and very slow, so that Thialfi soon gave up trying
to count them. In the evening they found a place under
an oak-tree where they could spend the night. Skrymir
gave them the wallet that they might have supper, but
he himself lay down at once to sleep and to snore.

' Thor took up the wallet to open it, but the knots in
the cord were as impossible to undo as the knots in a
stem of ivy. He lost his temper, and catching up the
hammer he struck the Giant a two-handed blow on the
head. Skrymir slowly awoke, looked round him and
said :

' " I think a leaf must have fallen on my head just
now. Something disturbed me. Have you had supper ?
I suppose I have been to sleep. When are you going
to lie down ? "

' " We are just thinking about it," said Thor, and with
that he found a place under the next tree and lay down.
But he could not sleep. The snoring of Skrymir was like
the grunting of a multitude of pigs ; it shook the leaves
on the tree overhead, and made the dead ones rise up
continually. At last Thor got up and struck the Giant
such a blow that the hammer was half buried in his
skull. This awakened the Giant, and he cried out :

' " What was that ? was it an acorn touched me on
the head ? Hullo, Thor, are you asleep ? "

' " No," said Thor, slipping away. " You woke me
up, Skrymir. It is only just midnight, and I shall go to
sleep again." He made up his mind that his next blow,
if the Giant went on snoring, should be a better one.
The snoring began again, and this time Thor hit the
Giant full in the face. Skrymir awoke and sat up,
stroking his cheek.

' " Are there any birds perched on this tree ? I think
some moss must have fallen on me. Hullo, Thor ! are

you awake ? It is about time for us to be getting up, I should think, though it is not far now to the city of Utgard. I have heard you whispering to one another that I am no Dwarf, not exactly a wren of men ; but when you come to Utgard you will see plenty of men taller than Skrymir. Therefore I advise you, when you are there, not to make too much of yourselves : the followers of Utgard-Loki will not stand any bragging from manikins like you, Thor. Perhaps the best thing for you would be to go back the way you have come, but if you will go on take that road to the east. My way is northward among those rocks."

' With these words Skrymir threw the wallet over his shoulders and strode away into the forest, and I never heard that Thor wanted to meet him again.

' The four now gave up all thought of sleep, and took the eastward road until towards noon they saw a city in the middle of the plain before them. It was still some way off, but so high were the buildings they had to bend their heads far back in order to see the tops. When they reached the walls the gateway was closed by a gate which was locked and bolted. Thor tried in vain to open it, but crept with little difficulty between the bars and entered the city with his companions. A large palace stood before them, and as the door was open they went in and saw a number of men sitting on benches in the hall. They were all bigger than Skrymir. The four travellers went up to the king of them and saluted him. The king took no notice of their salutes except to smile with contempt, and say to his companions :

' " That stripling must be Thor."

' Then turning to Thor he said :

' " Perhaps thou art taller than thou seemest. Canst

thou and thy friends show us any feats? We allow no one
here who cannot do something better than other men."

' " My feat," said Loki, " is to eat quicker than any
one else, as I will show you, if thou hast any one who will
race with me."

' " That will be a feat, if thou canst do as thou sayest,"
said Utgard-Loki. " Let us see." He then told one of
the men sitting at the far end of the bench, whose name
was Logi, to come forth and see whether he could
beat Loki. A trough full of meat was placed on the
floor : Loki stood at one end and Logi at the other,
and each began to eat as fast as he could, and the
one who reached the middle first was the winner. Logi
ate not only the flesh but the bones and the trough, yet
he was first at the middle. It was judged, therefore, that
Loki had been beaten.

' Utgard-Loki then asked if the young man with Thor
had any feat to perform. Thialfi said that he would run
a race with any one who came forward.

' " If thou canst win the race, that will be a feat
truly," said Utgard-Loki, " but we have some clever
runners here."

' The king and all the company now went to a plain
suitable for a running match, and called to a young
man named Hugi to race with Thialfi. Hugi ran round
once, and so far outstripped Thialfi that he had time
to turn round and meet him not far from the starting-
place.

' " Thou must ply thy legs better than that, Thialfi,"
said Utgard-Loki, " if thou meanest to win, though
I grant that I never saw an outsider run better. Try
again."

' In the second course Hugi beat Thialfi by a full bow
shot.

'"Thou runnest well," said Utgard, "but thou wilt hardly win, I think. The third course shall decide it."

'So they ran a third time, but Hugi was at the goal when Thialfi was only half-way round, and the spectators cried out that the match was at an end.

'Utgard-Loki next turned to Thor:

'"Now, Thor, how art thou going to show us that thy fame is deserved?"

'"I will drink with any one," said Thor.

'Utgard-Loki liked this proposal, and led the company back into the hall. There a large horn was brought which his men had to drain when they broke any of the rules of Utgard. The cup-bearer offered it to Thor, and Utgard-Loki said:

'"A good drinker will empty that horn at one draught. Some men will make two draughts of it, and I have seen some who can only finish it in three."

'Thor looked at it and thought it not a very great horn, though it was deep. He was thirsty, and he made little of it, so he set it to his lips. Without drawing breath he began to tilt the horn, and drank as deep as he could and set it down. But when he looked into it to see the bottom he saw only the dark liquor hardly at all diminished.

'"That is very well drunken," said Utgard-Loki, "though nothing much to boast of, and I should not have believed it if any one had told me that Thor could not take a bigger draught. But no doubt thou wilt show us what thou canst do at the second pull."

'Thor said nothing, but set his lips again to the horn and drank with all his might. Nevertheless, when he had to give up he saw that he had drunk rather less than before. The horn, however, could now be carried without spilling the drink.

' " How now, Thor ! " said Utgard-Loki, " thou must
not spare thyself. This is thy own particular feat,
remember. If thou wilt drain the horn at the third
draught thou must drink deep, and I must say that thy
fame will not be justified if thou showest no greater skill
in other feats than in this."

' Thor was angry, but he again put the horn to his
mouth and did his best to empty it. When he had come
to the end of his breath, however, he saw that there
was still plenty of drink left, and he gave back the horn
to the cup-bearer.

' " Well, well ! " said Utgard-Loki, " I see that thou
art not the man we thought thee. But is there any other
feat thou wilt try ? "

' " Yes ! " said Thor, " though such draughts as
I have taken would not have been reckoned small at
Asgard. Wilt thou propose another trial ? "

' " We have a pretty trifling game here," answered
Utgard-Loki, " which children play at. It is nothing
more than lifting my cat from the ground. I should
not have thought of mentioning it to Thor if I had not
already seen that thou art not the man that we took
thee to be."

' As he spoke a large grey cat ran in. Thor put his
hand under its middle and did his best to lift it up from
the floor, but the cat's back was only bent with all his
efforts ; only one of its feet was off the ground ; and
she purred during the whole of the trial. So Thor
gave it up.

' " That is as I expected," said Utgard-Loki : " the cat
is large, it is true, but Thor is little compared with us."

' " Ye call me little," said Thor, " but is there any one
here among ye that will wrestle with me now that I am
roused ? "

' " I see no one here," said Utgard-Loki, looking at his
men, " who would trouble to wrestle with such as thou ;
but let some one call my old nurse, Elli, and she shall
wrestle with thee. She has thrown many a man not less
mighty than Thor."

' This woman, who was old and toothless, now
entered the hall and came to grips with Thor. The more
he strained the firmer she stood. He struggled, began to
lose his foothold, and finally sank down on one knee.
Utgard-Loki said, " Enough ! It is no use going on,
Thor, and it is getting late." He showed Thor and his
companions to their seats, and they passed the night in
feasting.

' Next morning the four got ready to go. Utgard-
Loki came in and ordered a meal to be spread for them,
and they had abundance of food and drink. When
they had finished he led them to the gate of Utgard to
see them off. At parting he asked Thor what he
thought of the journey. Thor told him that he had
got nothing but shame by it. " It grieves me," he said,
" to think that ye will remember me as a man of little
worth."

' " No, no," said Utgard-Loki, " thou art mistaken.
What the truth of the matter is I will tell thee now that
thou hast left this city, which, so long as I live and can
have my way here, thou shalt never enter again. In fact,
if I had known beforehand how great thy strength was
and how near thou wouldst come to overthrowing me,
I should not have admitted thee at all. This is the truth.
I have been deceiving thee all this time by illusions and
things that are not what they seem. To begin with,
I am the Giant Skrymir, or rather the Giant Skrymir was
really me, Utgard-Loki. They were my knots, made
with iron wire, on the wallet which thou couldst not

undo. It was me thou didst strike with the hammer three times in the forest. The first of these blows was enough to have destroyed me, but though thou couldst not see it I placed a rocky mountain between me and thy hammer, and this I did to save me from each of the three blows. Search that mountain, and thou wilt find in its side three glens, one of them very deep, for it is the mark of thy third blow. I have deceived thee ever since in a similar way. Logi, with whom Loki competed in the eating match, was in reality fire itself: how then could Loki have won? Hugi, who ran with Thialfi in three races—and marvellously Thialfi ran—was Thought: is there anything swifter? Now take thy own performances. When thou didst try to empty the horn the feat was an amazing one, such as I should never have believed possible had I not seen it with my own eyes. For one end of the horn was in the sea all the time: if thou goest down to the shore thou wilt learn how much the sea has ebbed after those mighty draughts. The feat with the cat was also wondrous. When we saw thee lifting it so that one of its paws was off the floor, we were all filled with dread, and with good cause; for this cat was in reality the great serpent which encircles the whole of Midgard under the sea, and when thou hadst thy hand under him he could hardly keep his tail in his mouth, so high up was he lifted towards heaven: if his tail had come out of his mouth no one knows what would be the consequence. As to thy wrestling, that was the most astonishing feat of all. For the crone Elli, whom I called my old nurse, was Old Age; and there was never yet a man whom she will not sooner or later overthrow, and there never will be; but thou, Thor, came far nearer to throwing her down than any one else. Now farewell, Thor, and come not again, for if thou dost

I shall defend myself with other deceits, and thou never canst prevail against them."

' Thor was not to be flattered. All this time his rage had been increasing, and he lifted up his hammer at these last words to strike Utgard-Loki. But Utgard-Loki was not there. He looked for the city of Utgard, and it had disappeared : there was nothing left on the green plain for Thor to destroy. He could do nothing, therefore, but return home to his palace, vowing as he journeyed that he would make another attack on the Midgard serpent.'

VIII

THOR'S VICTORIES

'AND what,' asked Gangler, 'what came of Thor's
vow to make another attack on the Midgard serpent ? '

' It is,' said Har, ' no use concealing the fact from you.
Thor had no peace when he got back to Asgard. He
could think of nothing but Utgard and all his failures
there, particularly of the cat which was really the
Midgard serpent, the wolf's brother. He went about
striking the air with his hammer. "Why," they asked,
" dost thou strike at nothing, O Thor ? "

' " For an excellent reason," he replied; " because
Utgard-Loki has changed himself into nothing."

' But whether or not these blows did any harm to
Utgard-Loki no God knoweth. Before long Thor himself
tired of it, and left home secretly, without taking any
companion or even his goats and chariot. He put on the
likeness of a young man and so he travelled until dark,
when he came to the dwelling of Hymir, one of the Giants.
He saluted the Giant and asked for a night's lodging,
which was readily granted to him, because the house was
huge and he was small. At break of day, when he saw
Hymir making ready his boat for fishing, he got up
and begged the Giant to let him come on board and
take an oar.

' " A shrivelling such as thou art would not be much
use," said the Giant. " Besides, thou wilt catch thy death
of cold out there, if I stay as long as usual."

' " I am not afraid of that," said Thor. " I will go

out as far as thou wishest, and perhaps it will not be
I that will want to turn back again." He was very
nearly attacking the Giant there and then, but he kept
himself in hand because he had other fish to fry at
that time.

' " What bait shall we use, Hymir ? " he said, as if he
were thinking of nothing else.

' " Find your own bait," answered the Giant.

' Thor found his own bait. He ran up from the shore
to where the Giant's cattle were feeding, and picking
out the largest bull, which was coal-black, he wrung off
its head and carried it down to the boat without a word.
Hymir made a wry face when he saw the black bull's
head, but he said nothing. They then put out to sea.
Each of them had two oars, and the God pulled so that
they could feel the boat being lifted along, which
astonished the Giant very much.

' " That will do," said Hymir; " this is a good place
for flounders."

' " Oh no," said Thor, " we will go on a good bit farther
than this while we are about it ; " and he continued
to row.

' They went on for a great distance, and Thor showed
no signs of being satisfied, when Hymir called out :

' " Easy now, my lad; if thou art not careful we shall
be alongside the Midgard serpent, and then we shall
know it. We shall both be provided for."

' Thor took no notice whatever, but rowed on and on
until he thought fit to stop. At last he did so, and laid
down his oars. Both began to fish, and at first Hymir
had all the sport. He was always either throwing out
his line or pulling it in again with a whale, and often two
whales, at the end. Thor had taken out a fishing-line
and hook of suitable size, and cast it far out to sea

with the bull's head for a bait. For a long time his line
hung loose and curved in the water, and Thor watched
Hymir. At last the line straightened out and grew stiff.
and tight. And now it may be said with truth that
Thor deceived the Midgard serpent as thoroughly as it
had deceived him at Utgard. The monster let go of his
tail and caught greedily at the bait, and would have
swallowed it had not the hook caught fast in his jaw.
The pain made the serpent shake his head, and the
shaking of his head caused the boat to rock to and fro.
Thor had to hold on to the line with all his might. Once
he loosened his grasp for an instant, and, gripping the
line as it was running out, he was dragged to the edge
and his knuckles all skinned against the gunwale.
If he could have had sport like this every day, he
thought, when he had got over this slip, he would have
been a fisherman all his life. The Giant, on the other
hand, would willingly have changed places with Thor at
any other time : at that moment he wished either that
Thor was at the bottom of the sea or that he himself
was at home. It seemed, however, unlikely that Thor
would go to the bottom, unless he took the boat and the
Giant with him. Thor was pulling his hardest, and the
serpent was doing the same, and with the pressure of
the God's feet against the bottom of the boat the planks
were creaking. At last they creaked still more, cracked,
splintered, and altogether gave way. Thor's feet went
clean through to the bottom of the sea, and as he now
had firmer foothold he was able to haul the serpent up
to the edge of the boat, and its dark head stuck out
through the foam with which it had covered the sea
like froth on ale. Thor looked at the serpent with equal
anger and satisfaction ; his eyes flashed with crystal
flames ; and once he struck the monster on the ear

with his fist. The serpent replied by spirting venom. Hymir had nothing to do but to expect the worst, unless indeed the serpent would swallow Thor and leave him his boat. But as this seemed very unlikely the Giant had to act for himself. Thor was just about to strike the serpent on the head with his hammer when the Giant cut the line. The blow fell, but whether it fell faster than the serpent no one has yet decided. Some assert that the hammer reached the serpent under the water and struck off its head. Others are equally certain that the serpent is still alive at the bottom of the sea. The only person who knows is the one who recovered the hammer. Those who believe that the serpent is alive, and those who believe that he is not, agree on one thing : that the hook is in the serpent's jaw, alive or dead. But if the fate of the Midgard serpent is unknown, that of the Giant Hymir is well known, because Thor told it himself, In anger at losing the serpent, Thor struck the owner of the boat a blow that sent him into the sea, and from there to a place where they have no boats and no need of them. Thor himself, pulling his legs out of the holes of the boat, waded to the land, returned to Asgard and told the story which you have now heard.'

' Dost thou think,' asked Gangler, ' that the serpent swallowed the bullock's head after all ? '

' It never occurred to me to think about it,' said Har.

' But now that thou dost think about it, what is thy opinion ? ' persisted Gangler.

' I do not know,' answered Har, ' but this I know, that questions are easier than answers, except to me, for I never ask questions.'

' Now that thou hast told him that story of Hymir,' said Jafnhar, ' I will tell him the other story of Thor and Hymir. Perhaps this Hymir was another Giant of the same name: at any rate, as I know the story Thor did not kill him.

‘ The Gods were going away after their first feast in the hall of Eager, the Sea Giant. The guests had been too many and too grand for Eager, and he was glad to see them go ; he was a simple fellow, and it was quite plain to see that he was glad. But Thor did not like to see a man smiling with the pleasure of getting rid of him ; so he said :

‘ “ We shall come back again soon, Eager, and often too. Your smile does me good.”

‘ “ I did not ask you,” said Eager, “ but if you come, you can bring with you a cauldron big enough to brew ale for the lot of you. I haven’t one.”

‘ “ Oh, certainly,” said Thor, thinking it an easy thing. But it was not. None of the Gods knew of such a cauldron. It was from Tyr that he heard of one at last. Said Tyr :

‘ “ My grim father Hymir is the man. He lives east of the Sleet Bays, at the ends of heaven, and he has a cauldron a mile deep.”

‘ “ Can we get it ? ” asked Thor.

‘ “ Yes,” said Tyr, “ but we shall have to think of a way.”

‘ “ The two together rode a long day’s journey, and put up the goats at Egil’s house. Egil was Tyr’s uncle. Then they went on to Hymir’s hall. Tyr’s grandmother was there, an old woman with nine hundred heads, whom Tyr did not like at all. But presently his mother came out, and she was a grand woman. She offered Tyr a beer-cup, saying :

‘ “ Child of Giants ! I will hide you two adventurers under the cauldron. Father is often sharp and savage with his guests.”

' Therefore they hid themselves under one of the eight
cauldrons on a high shelf in the hall. Hymir came
home late from hunting. Icicles clattered at the end
of his chin-thicket—or beard, as you would say—and he
had a toothache.

' " Good evening, Hymir ! " said his wife. " Don't be
angry. Thy son has come, whom we have long been
looking for. He has brought with him the Giant Killer—
you know—the friend of man, I should say. There
they are up there on the shelf, behind the pillar."

' The Giant turned to look at them, and at the mere
look the shelf gave way and down fell eight cauldrons.
Thor and Tyr were left with no cover at all, close to the
Giant : he was looking hard at Thor, for he could not
expect any good from him who makes Giantesses widows.
But for the present nothing happened except that Hymir
ordered three oxen to be killed and put in the pot to
boil, for he was fond of boiled beef. Thor, however, ate
all three before he fell asleep. As he left the bones,
and the heads had been cut off before boiling, Hymir
did not starve, though he said :

' " We three shall want supper again to-morrow,
I suppose."

' Thor said he would like a day's fishing. What
happened Thor must have known. You have heard one
story, that tells how he nearly caught the Midgard
serpent who escaped because Hymir cut the line, and
how he pitched the Giant into the sea for his pains.
But this story says that Hymir caught whales and Thor
lost the serpent, and thus they came home together.
When they landed Hymir said :

' " Now do your part. Either carry the whales up or
house the ship."

' Thor stepped forward and caught up the ship under

one arm and carried it, with the whales in it, up the steep
pathway among the rocks to where the Giant lived.

'At supper that evening they were talking about feats
of strength. The Giant was not willing to admit that
Thor was stronger than ordinary. " A man may pull
a good oar as Thor does, but what I should call a strong
man is one who could break this vat, now."

'At this he tapped the vat with his knuckles. Thor
took it up and threw it with all his might, so that it
broke through one of the pillars ; but the vat itself was
brought back to him unbroken. He threw it a second
time, and the same thing happened. " I will tell you what
to do," whispered the Giant's lady : " dash it down on
Hymir's skull ; it is harder than the vat." Thor acted
on this advice. He moved along the bench towards
his host, as if to throw in another direction, and then
swinging the vat overhead, instead of letting it go, he
brought it down on the back of the Giant's skull. The
vat was broken ; the skull remained as before, except
that it was full of regret for the good wine which ran out
of the broken vat on to the floor. The Giant was half
crying over the waste of wine. Then he thought of
another test for the strength of Thor. " Can you carry
my ale cauldron out of the hall ? " said he.

' " Very gladly," said Thor. Tyr was the first to
try, but he could not even lift up its rim, which lay on
the floor as it had fallen from the shelf. Thor drove
his feet through the floor before he could fairly raise
up the cauldron, which he then put on his head like
a hat. The pothooks rattled about his head as he
walked off with it out of the hall. As he remained
outside for some time, Hymir, who had forgotten him for
the moment and had been looking at the wine-vat, got
up to see what was happening, half hoping to find Thor

buried under the cauldron.   Instead of which, he saw
the two already mounting on Thor's chariot with the
cauldron.   He called together his fellow Giants and
started in pursuit.   Many of them got near enough to
Thor to be killed by his hammer, but none got any nearer.
And thus Thor brought home a cauldron large enough
for Eager to brew drink for all the Gods.   They say that
Thor drinks ale at Eager's once every harvest-time.'

IX

THOR'S VICTORIES (*continued*)

THEN said Gangler:

' Thor must have killed many a Giant. Whenever he was swinging his hammer there seems to have been a Giant's head in the way of it. Yet I cannot understand why the Giants did not join together to destroy him. They knew his habits perfectly well. Old Hymir, for example, addressed him as the one who makes Giantesses widows. Why, then, did they not make an end of Thor ? '

' They were unable to,' said Har.

' But why ? ' asked Gangler.

' Something prevented them,' answered Har.

' And what was that something ? Was it the Norns, or what ? '

' I do not know, except that such is the fact.'

' Had he any more adventures among Giants ? '

' Many. I will tell you one more, and it is remarkable because Thor was without his own hammer, belt, and gauntlets.'

' How was that ? '

' It was Loki's fault. He was flying hither and thither as he often did, wearing Freya's hawk-skin, purely for a pastime, and catching sight of Garfred's garth he flew that way. When he saw the hall he descended and perched at a window to look in. Garfred the Giant was sitting inside in great comfort, but looked up and saw a bird ; and he told a man to catch the bird. The man was some time climbing up the wall,

which was both high and difficult. Loki looked on,
thinking it sport to see the man taking so much trouble
all for nothing. He stayed until the last moment before
flying away, and when he spread his wings he found that
his talons were already fast in the hands of the man. He
had got sleepy with watching the slow climb, and so he was
caught and taken to the Giant Garfred. When he looked
into the hawk's eyes Garfred thought that it was really
a man—for no bird ever had eyes as clever as Loki's
or as wicked—and he said : " There is a man's spirit
behind this hawk's plumage. Who are you ? " Loki
made no reply. The Giant was not deceived, and instead
of setting the bird free he shut it up in a chest, to see
whether starvation would sharpen its wit and give it
a voice. And so it did. In three months' time Loki
would have said anything in the hope of getting free.
Garfred had him taken out of the chest, and bade him
talk. Loki declared at once who he was, and said that
he wished to be set free.

'" What will you do if I set you free ? " asked
Garfred.

'" What do you want ? " asked Loki.

'" You are very obliging," said Garfred. " Now what
I should like most of all is to have Thor here without his
hammer, without his belt, and without his mittens.
I want to discover whether the hammer, the belt, and
the mittens are what makes Thor so powerful and
famous ; whether he is anything at all by himself."

'" I will do what you wish," said Loki, and he was set
free. After eating and drinking, he set off to Asgard,
and when he met Thor he told him a tale :

'" Thor," he said, " I have just come from a Giant's
palace, where they showed me a most curious thing
which they called Thor."

' " A thing ? " said Thor.

' " Yes, and not a very big thing. It belongs to the Giant Garfred, who is very old and has this one joke. When anybody comes to see him he says, ' You did not notice Thor.' "

' " ' Thor ? ' " says the guest, in some alarm.

' " ' Oh, you may well be afraid of the thing,' says Garfred; ' there it is, and now you may say that you have seen Thor and found him not a very terrible fellow.' "

' " And what is *it* ? " asked Thor.

' " It is a hammer with a gauntlet on each end and a girdle round the middle. Garfred says that those are Thor, and that without them you are nothing. At least, he says that he has never heard any proof to the contrary."

' " Where is Garfred's garth ? " asked Thor.

' " I will show you. It is a smooth, easy way."

' And so they set out. It was not smooth or easy, but Thor was in a hurry. They stayed one night with a Giantess named Grith. Thor had met her before, and since he had made her a widow. He did not know that she lived here, and was delighted to see her again. He told her his errand, how he was going to teach Garfred who Thor was. " But where is your hammer ? where is your belt ? where are the gauntlets ? "

' " That is the point," said Thor. " I am going without them, to show that Thor is not made by his hammer, belt, and gauntlets."

' " But if I were you," said the good widow, " I would take something. I can lend you a pair of gauntlets, a belt, and an oak staff. You will be quite safe with them."

' " Safe ! " said Thor, angrily.

' " I mean," she said, " that these things are very useful, though of course they are nothing like your own. Garfred is a clever sort of giant, and very thickset. You may just as well keep your hands clean. Then the staff will be handy in crossing the rivers farther on. This girdle, again, takes up no room and looks well."

' Thor did not thank her for the gifts, but took them with him next morning. He and Loki had to cross many a swollen river as full of tumbling stones as of water coming down from the mountains, rolling even the slippery round boulders which the Gods were scrambling on. The worst river of all was Wimmer. Before Thor had got to the middle of it the water was beating upon his shoulders. He was glad enough then of the girdle, which seemed to him to give strength like his own girdle. Loki clung to it and got nothing worse than a wetting. The staff supported him against the moving wall of waters. Working his way across, he cried :

' " Do your worst, Wimmer. I am wading through to Giantland, and will not be stopped. The higher you rise the greater will be my strength and the deeper your shame."

' As he stood still balancing himself almost in midstream, he caught sight of a Giant maiden, Gialp, one of Garfred's daughters. She was in a glen close by, making the river rise by means of spells. So Thor took a great stone out of the river and cast it at her. Thor never missed what he aimed at. The water began to sink, and he made his way steadily to the bank. A certain rowan-tree overhung the water, and grasping it he climbed up on to the land, at a little distance from Garfred's hall. They were shown first into the goat-house, and Thor supposed that this was because he was unrecognized ; for he had no suspicion that Loki had decoyed him there to keep the oath he had sworn. Thor was sitting down on a stool, waiting for something to happen, when he felt the stool and himself being reared up towards the roof. He would have gone through it, if he had not used the rod of Grith in time. He held the point of it against the roof and pressed hard so as to thrust the stool back again. Slowly the stool began to descend, but not at all smoothly, and at last something cracked and a great shriek was heard, and the stool fell to the ground. Thor fell on his feet, and there under the stool he saw the Giant's daughters, with their backs broken.

' It seemed to Thor time for him to be going into the hall, and as he was starting a messenger met him, asking him to come. He followed the messenger into the hall, which was a cave lighted by a forge fire and by the eyes of Giants sitting round it.

' " Who are you ? " said Garfred, the chief of the Giants.

' " Thor," said Thor, and the Giants roared with laughter.

' " Where are your hammer, belt, and gauntlets ? Thor is not Thor without them."

' " I left them in Asgard," said Thor, " knowing that I was coming to a place where I should be safe enough, but where those precious things might be stolen."

' " Hail, Thor ! " said Garfred, and took up from the forge a bar of iron so hot that it burnt the eyes of the Giants and they dripped tears on to the stones at their feet. He swung this burning bar at Thor with all his might. The faces of a thousand Giants watching were lighted up by it for a moment like rows of moons, as it rushed through the hall. Thor waited for it and caught it in the iron gauntlets. His face shone like Balder's

as he held it, but the Giants knew well that it was Thor.
He smiled, thinking of Grith and her counsel. Then he
hurled back the bar. Garfred was hidden behind one of
the pillars of the hall, but the bar found him out through
the pillar ; it pierced his body and then the wall behind.
The broken pillar fell upon the remains of the Giant
and the roof followed, catching fire from the forge.
The crowd of Giants were now mad with fear, between
the fire at one end and Thor invisible at the other.
Many rushed into the fire. Some of those who were
undecided were knocked down by the rush ; others were
hustled and began to fight amongst themselves ; and
now here, now there, Thor and the rod of Grith made
themselves felt without being seen. There was anger
and there was fear among the Giants, but there was no
courage. One moment a Giant would be shrieking with
fear because he thought Thor was behind him ; the
next moment, finding that he was safe, he was bellowing
with anger at the Giant in front of him for having been
in his way ; and then the two fought until they were
separated by a common fear of the destroyer. Thor
slew those who stood up ; the rest were trampled to
death or slew one another. The fire was quenched in the
blood. The victory was Thor's ; yet he had fought with
no help from Miolnir, or the belt, or the gauntlets.'

'What about Grith's rod, and her belt and her
gauntlets ? ' said Gangler.

' They were not the same thing,' said Har.

X

GODS AND GODDESSES

' ALL thy tales,' said Gangler, ' are of Odin or Thor
or Loki. Have the other Gods ever done anything except
rule the world with the help of the Norns ? '

' It is not lawful to tell everything about the Gods
to a man,' said Har.

' I should like to hear what is lawful, if it is worth
hearing.'

' I will tell thee of some Anses and some Wanes, for
those are the two races of Gods. For a long time they
were at war and fought many battles, but they made
peace at last, after both sides had won victories. To
make the peace good each side spat into a jar. Out
of this the Gods made a being whom they called Kvasir ;
he was made so wise that no one could ask him a question
which he could not answer. Kvasir travelled over the
whole world to teach men wisdom, but was murdered
at length by two Dwarfs. They killed him because they
believed they would thus be able to get at all his wisdom
instead of having only what he chose to give. If he could
give wisdom, they said, he must have it ; and if he has
it, it must be inside him, for he goes from place to place
with nothing else but his clothes. So they drained
Kvasir's blood and mixed it with honey. Whoever
drinks of this blood and honey becomes a poet. The
Dwarfs did not long keep the secret to themselves.
They gave out that Kvasir had been choked by his own
too great wisdom, because he had not been asked enough

questions. But instead of living quietly on wisdom
and blood and honey, they killed a Giant and his wife
who had no wisdom.   Their son, whose name was Suttung, took revenge on the Dwarfs.   He carried them
out to sea, and then left them on a sandbank which was
covered at high tide.   They begged him to set them free,
offering to pay him with the drink that makes poets.
Suttung, though a Giant, agreed to this, and gave the
precious goblet to the care of his daughter Gunnlauth.
Poetry is sometimes called Kvasir's blood, Suttung's
mead, or the Dwarfs' ransom.

' But this mead did not long remain with the Giants.
Odin himself went on a journey alone to Giantland to
gain it.   As he journeyed he came to a meadow where
nine men were mowing.   He said " Good morning ",
and had a talk with them about mowing.   He knew the
best way to sharpen a scythe, he said, and offered to
sharpen theirs.   This they gladly allowed him to do.
When he had finished they found that their scythes
would cut grass as if it were air, and they begged him
to sell the whetstone.   Instead of selling it, Odin threw
the whetstone up into the air for them to scramble for it.
But they were so eager to catch it that they did not put
down their scythes.   The result was that they all killed
one another with the blades.   Odin left them there, and
put up for the night with Suttung's brother, Baugi,
who was complaining how he had lost nine men in one
day, and had no one to finish cutting his hay.   Odin,
who went by the name of Baulverk, offered to take
the place of the nine men, if he might have a drink of
Suttung's mead at the end of his work.   Baugi promised
that he should, and Odin stayed with him until the end
of the hay harvest, working hard.   Baugi now went to
get the mead from his brother ; but Suttung would not

let him have one drop. ' Odin therefore made up his
mind to go himself to the cavern where Gunnlauth
kept it. This cavern had no entrance anywhere. But
Baugi bored a hole in the rock, and Odin crept through
it in the form of a worm. Once inside, he became a
God again, and stood before the solitary and astonished
Gunnlauth. She could not refuse him ; she offered him
a draught from each of the three jars where the mead
was stored ; and he drank so deep that not a drop was
left in any one of them. · Thanking Gunnlauth and bidding her farewell, he crawled out again from the cavern.
Once outside, he took the form of an eagle in order to
escape as swiftly as possible. Suttung was not long in
discovering the trick, and followed him in the form of
another eagle. The Gods watched the race from the rocks
of Asgard. As soon as Odin alighted they brought out
jars, which he filled through his beak. This is the true
draught of poets, and poetry is sometimes called Odin's
booty, Odin's gift, or the drink of the Gods.'

'But thou wast speaking of Anses and Wanes,' said
Gangler.

'Odin is the chief of the Anses, and all his children
and descendants are Anses, all of the Gods in fact,
except Frey and Freya and their father Niord, who are
Wanes. Niord was originally sent to Asgard as a
hostage, but he never returned to the Wane-world where
he was born. His kingdom is Noatun, which is in
heaven. He is a kindly God, without guile. He rules the
winds, so far as he can, and checks the fury of the sea
and of fire. Fishermen particularly pray to Niord. He
has treasures without end, and makes rich some of those
who pray to him. When a man is rich it is said that
" Frey and Niord have blessed him with a store of
wealth ". Niord married Skadi, daughter of Thiassi,

one of the Mountain Giants. She wished always to live among the mountains where she was born, and Niord went for a time to live there with her. But he liked the sea best ; he became sad among the mountains, where he heard wolves instead of swans. So it was agreed that he and his wife should spend nine days in the mountains and then three by the sea. But Skadi could not sleep for the screaming of the sea-birds, and she left the sea and went back again to the mountains. There she is happy in her father's old house, or chasing the wild beasts with her bow and arrows over the snow. Niord is a gentle God. No one was insulted worse than he by Loki when the Gods were feasting after the death of Balder. Loki scoffed at him for being a Wane, and Niord answered : " It is my comfort that though I came here as a hostage, yet I had a son here whom no one hates, and who is best of the Anses."

'This son of Niord is the God who is called " the bright Frey ", the blessed son of Niord. He is also called " the bright slayer of Beli " because he once slew a great Giant of that name. He is the God of rain and sunshine and of all the fruits of the earth, and he dwells in Elfheim. Men who wish to have good harvests and to preserve or gain peace, offer prayers to Frey. Like his father Niord, he gives men riches. He rides sometimes a horse called Bloodyhoof, sometimes a boar with golden tusks, which he was riding at Balder's funeral. Frey has lost his sword, and will be without it when the last battle is fought. There is a tale which explains this.

'His mother Skadi had noticed that for some time Frey had been moody and silent. Thinking he must be angry about something, she asked Skirni, his old friend, if he knew what was the matter. But Skirni said that if he said a word to him Frey blazed up in a fury. However, Skadi persuaded him to go again.

' " Tell me, O Frey, thou captain of the Gods," said Skirni, " why thou, my lord, sittest all day long alone in thy hall."

' " How can I tell thee, my lad, this heavy sorrow ? The sun shines day by day, but brings me no joy."

' " Can thy grief be too great to tell me, Frey, though we have known one another since we were boys ? "

' " I went up into Lidskialf the other day and looked over the world, and towards the north I saw a maid crossing Gymir's field. Whether it was her beauty which lighted up the sea with its brightness, or whether it was being on Odin's throne, I have been sad ever since. I love her, but neither the Gods nor the Elves will let us be together."

' Skirni asked Frey to lend him his sword and his horse which would go through fire, and then rode away. In his dark ride over the boggy hills of Ogreland, Skirni kept up his courage by talking to the horse. At last he saw a Giant shepherd sitting on a mound, and asked how he could see the maid in spite of Gymir's hounds. The shepherd thought he must be mad or else a ghost, to think of such a thing. Skirni answered that he was not afraid, but in great haste. With the shepherd's help he found the hall of Gymir. Gerda was inside sitting down, while a bondmaid was at work. She heard him clattering in the court. " What is that clattering clatter ? " said she. " It is a man. He is getting off his horse. The horse is grazing now," said the bondmaid. " Go," said Gerda, " invite him into the hall to refresh himself with some of our clear mead." She was small, and rather dark than fair ; she was merry and contented, but with fits of bad temper because the bondmaid, her

only companion, was stupid. When Skirni came in she
said in astonishment :

' " Which one of the sons of the Gods can this be ?
How ever didst thou get over the huge fire outside, young
man ? "

' " I am not one of the Gods," said Skirni, " though
I did get through thy fire. I have come with these
eleven apples of gold to win thy love for Frey."

' " I will not have thy eleven apples," said she, " never;
not for any one's love ; nor will I ever love Frey, with
or without his apples."

' " I will give thee Balder's ring, that yields eight other
rings exactly like it every ninth night."

' " I want no rings, whether they were taken from
Balder's body or not. We have plenty of gold here."

' Skirni hesitated. Gerda laughed at him. This made
up his mind for him.

' " Look on this blade," he said, showing her the
sword, " I will cut thy head off with it, unless thou change
thy mind."

' Gerda knew well enough that he would do nothing
of the kind, though she disliked the look of the sword.
" I am not going to be driven to love any man," she said,
" and if thou and Gymir meet, it will be his turn to
threaten."

' " Not so," said Skirni, " but I will keep this sword for
the old man. I have a magic wand that will be better for
thee. It will send thee where no man can see thee, but the
Giants will; and there thou shalt sit on a mound looking
towards Hell. Thou shalt loathe thy meat, and yet thou
shalt eat it because thou hast not the courage to die."

' Gerda was going to slip away. For he said it in such
a way that she believed it. But she could not escape,
and he went on :

' " The demons shall pinch thee every day in Giant-land. Thou shalt never know what love is, though maybe thou shalt have a three-headed monster for a husband. Yet thou shalt linger on and on like a dead thistle. The Gods hate thee. Even Frey shall hate thee. Come here, ye Giants! ye Frost Giants! and all ye Gods! come and hear me swear that Gerda shall never be loved again."

' Gerda would have cried had she been alone, but instead of that she fetched a goblet and offered it to Skirni, saying:

' " Hail now, lad, and take this cup of old mead!"

' Skirni was thirsty with his anger, and drank it up. Gerda watched him. Presently she spoke, half to herself:

' " I never thought to love one of the Anses."

' Skirni caught her up:

' " But I must have an answer to take back. When wilt thou meet the bright son of Niord?"

' " In three days' time," she answered, " at Barra."

' " Good," said he, " now that is sensible. I should like to drink thy health in another goblet of that excellent mead." The goblet was filled and filled again, and yet a third time, before he rode away singing. Frey saw him from afar off and cried out, asking for the news. When he heard it he did not even thank Skirni, but went away into a solitary place and raved because he had three days to wait. Yet those three days passed away, and Gerda was true to her promise. But he never had back his sword, and that is why he had to slay Beli with a stag's horn. He will miss the sword in earnest when the sons of Muspell march against the Gods.'

' Tell me about Frey's sister, Freya,' said Gangler.

' First I will tell thee about Frigga, Odin's wife, though as she is very grand there is not much to say about her.

She keeps to her own home and has no adventures. Yet she is so renowned that Odin is sometimes called " Frigga's husband " or " Frigga's love ". She was the mother of Balder, and she lives at Fensaler.

' Freya is a very great Goddess, and her palace is called Folkvang. She shares the dead with Odin. Half go to her and half to him. Sometimes she flies in her chequered hawk-dress of feathers : sometimes she rides in a car drawn by two cats. She first taught the Gods enchantments, which she learnt from the Wanes. Her chief adventure was when she did not go to be the bride of the Giant Thrym, which I have already told. The Giant exclaimed : " Look, Giants, stand up and look. They are bringing me my wife, Freya, the daughter of Niord of Noatun." But he was mistaken, and more than disappointed, for he was shortly slain. Freya is married, but her husband, whose name is Odur, left her to travel into a very distant country, where he has remained. He left behind him one beautiful daughter, named Hnossa. Freya is sad and often weeps. But she is still beautiful, and her necklace, called Brising, is the most famous of all necklaces. She weeps for loss of love, but she is fond of hearing love-songs, and listens kindly to prayers when lovers make them.

' Lofna is another Goddess who is mild and gracious, particularly to lovers, and her name means love and whatsoever is lovely and lovable.

' Vora is the Goddess who listens to all oaths, and punishes those that break them. Nothing is hidden from her.

' There is Sif also, who is the wife of Thor. She thought to escape Loki's tongue at the banquet by offering him a cup of mead ; but he took the mead, and she got the insult in spite of it.

'And there are many other Goddesses, but the more like Gods and the less like human beings they are, the less there is to say about them.'

'Tell me,' said Gangler, 'about the other Gods.'

'I have spoken of Tyr. He alone of the Gods cares to feed Fenrir the wolf, and it was he who made sure of fettering the wolf and lost his hand for his pains. He is as brave as Thor; perhaps braver, for he has not Thor's strength, having only one hand. A one-handed man is often called a Tyr. He gives courage to men, and it is a good thing for a warrior to pray to Tyr. He makes up for his lack of Thor's strength by great wisdom, and a wise man is said to be as wise as Tyr, while a valiant man is said to be as valiant as Tyr. It was he that told Thor where he could find the cauldron big enough to brew ale for all the Gods.

'There is Heimdall, who is also called the White God. His palace is Himinbiorg, which is at the end of the bridge Bifrost. He guards this bridge, and is called the glad watchman of the Gods. Few others would be glad in that solitary, remote, and dangerous position. He will be the first to be attacked by the sons of Muspell. But until then he sits drinking the goodly mead in the peaceful hall of Himinbiorg, which is as peaceful as the grave. Loki taunted him with having a dull life and a wet back. But he is so contented, and so loves mead, that he does not feel either the dullness or the wet back. His back is wet with going out from time to time to look over towards Giantland. Others call him foolish, but those who do so could never do his work. They would either leave it or go mad, both foolish things. Heimdall needs less sleep than a bird, and mead cannot make him drowsy. He sees a hundred miles around him by night or day. He can hear whatever sound there is, even to the grass growing in the earth, and the wool growing on a sheep's back. He keeps a horn in the hall, and some day he will blow it.

' There is Vidar, surnamed the Silent, the son of Thor and Grith. He wears thick shoes made out of all the shreds of leather thrown away by shoemakers ; so that these shreds are not wasted as men suppose. He is very strong. It was Vidar who made way for Loki at the banquet where he insulted everybody. It is said of him and another God, Wali, that they will inhabit the city of the Gods when the fire of Surtur is quenched.

' Ullur is another God. He is supreme in archery and skating. He is handsome and a good warrior. Were he not a God he would be a fine man, but as he is a God he will live for ever, or until Ragnarok.

' There is also Bragi, the God who is a poet and has a beautiful wife. Another is Forseti, the son of Balder and Nanna. He lives in the mansion called Glitnir, and he is such a judge that all who bring their cases to him for trial go away content. He himself is at peace and he gives peace to men.'

' How ? ' asked Gangler.

' At Glitnir thou mayest answer that question thyself.'

' I am too old to go to Glitnir,' said Gangler, but Har did not hear.

XI

THE APPLES OF YOUTH, AND THE DAY
OF DOOM

' Who is Bragi's beautiful wife ? ' asked Gangler, not
because he wished to know, but because he hoped to
keep up the conversation and learn something of
importance.

' Her name,' said Har, ' is Iduna. She is one of the
eight Goddesses who sit in hall with the twelve Gods.
She is the loveliest and the youngest, and by her appearance she seems always to be nineteen years old ; and
needless to say that as she looks so young she is also
wise. She has a secret which none of the other Gods has
ever learnt, nor, I think, has she—the secret of everlasting happiness. She is called the sorrow-healing
Maiden. She keeps the Gods' Elixir of Youth, and if
she lost it or refused to give it to them they would at once
feel the weight of all the ages of their lives : their backs
would bend, their hair would grow grey and fall out,
and their eyes would be like shellfish and good for nothing
except to see causes for misery. This elixir is the juice
of certain apples which Iduna alone possesses. They
look like ordinary apples, and she gathers them off an
old apple-tree in a wood full of such trees. Others have
stolen into the wood and taken away many apples, but
never any like Iduna's, though they look and taste well
enough. Yet Iduna will take a God out with her into
the wood and pick an apple for one without any secrecy.
Possibly it is Iduna's own touch that gives her apples

this power of healing sorrow and renewing youth.
I do not know. . . .'

'I wonder,' said Gangler to himself, 'if a beautiful
woman's touch could have such power?' He remembered the day when he thought it could. He and his
men had sailed far away among the islands of the West
fighting and plundering, and at last they had landed in
Wales. All day they fought among the grey rocks and
grey trees at the foot of a mountain whose top they
never saw for mist. The brook a little below them ran
silent because of the dead men that had fallen into it over
the rocks. But at last they could not see the enemy any
more, and at evening they came to where the brook
ran into a broad river. The two waters almost encircled
an orchard, and the last light of the sun was shining on
the trees, which were the oldest Gangler had ever seen.
Their twigs were so dense, and the lichen was so furry on
the twigs, that each tree looked like a magpie's nest,
except that it was spotted with golden apples. There
was a girl gathering the apples, and she looked at Gangler
and his men carelessly, as men look at animals, without
kindness or unkindness, and she tossed apples over the
river, and laughed to see the strange men picking them
up. But because one of the men leapt into the water
to go to her she slipped away among her trees. The man
searched for her in vain. None of them saw her any
more. So when the man who had swum over came
back, the king slew him in a great fit of anger. A cold
wind blew, and the mist from the mountains hid the
orchard. Gangler sighed as he heard the voice of Har
saying:

'There is no one whom the Gods would miss more than
Iduna, and they never felt so much shame as when Loki
spoke vilely to her.

' Loki was the cause of her only woe. He and Odin and another once took a journey together. They went over the wildest hills and through the darkest forests, and it was not long before they were without food. When, therefore, they caught sight of a herd of oxen feeding in one of the greener dales among the hills, they were not slow in killing one. They lit a fire and put the ox in a pot over the fire to stew. When Loki thought it should be done he tried it, but found it far from ready. They gave it another hour before they tried it again, and it was as raw as before. Yet the fire was good enough. Then they began to talk about the matter, to get at the cause of this strange thing. As they talked they heard a voice overhead in an oak-tree, and the voice said that he knew the reason why the ox-flesh was not cooked. They looked up and saw that it was an old eagle, and not a little one, sitting in the oak. Said the eagle : " If ye will give me my fill of the ox the meat will be done," and though he was a great eagle they consented to give him his fill. As soon as he heard them say " Yes " he came down for his share, since he had no liking for cooked meat. He seized one thigh and both shoulders of the ox, and would have flown up to his perch with them. But Loki had a quick eye for the knavery of others. Moreover he had been looking after the fire, so, snatching up a great stick, he struck the bird with all his might across the back. The eagle rose up in the air with the stick fast in his back at one end and in Loki's hands at the other. Loki could not get free, and was dragged along over the tops of trees and rocks until he thought that his legs would be broken off and his arms torn from his shoulders. He did not suffer any the less because he was fat. He cried out to be set free, but the eagle said that Loki should never be free unless he

brought Iduna and her apples at a certain time out of
Asgard. Loki, who would have promised anything,
consented, although he knew well that the eagle was
really the Giant Thiazzi. He was set free and he
returned to his companions, boasting that he had out-
witted the eagle, but saying nothing about his promise.

' When they got back to Asgard, Loki waited until
the appointed time and then persuaded Iduna to
come out into a wood where he said that he had found
some apples equal to her own. " Bring some of thine
with thee, Iduna," he said, " so that we may compare
them together." Iduna smiled at this, for, she said, " My
apples are known by their powers, not their looks, and
their powers no one has ever doubted." " That is
true, Iduna," said Loki, " but nevertheless bring some
of thine, because these in the wood seem to me to be of
the same shape and colour as well as the same power."
Iduna was not to be deceived, yet took some apples with
her to avoid Loki's nasty tongue. But when they were
in the wood down flew the Giant Thiazzi and picked
her up with the apples and carried her off. The hoary
Giants of the rocks were glad when Iduna came amongst
them.

' In Asgard the Gods missed her at once. The sun
was not the same thing now that Iduna was gone:
nothing was the same. They began to feel their age,
and they called a council to consider what had happened
and what should be done. It came out at once that
Iduna had last been seen entering the wood with Loki.
Loki was brought before them, and as they threatened
him with torture he promised to bring back Iduna. He
borrowed Freya's hawk-skin and flew off to Giantland.
Thiazzi was not at home, but fishing out at sea. Iduna
was alone in the house, so that it was easy for Loki to

change her into the convenient shape of a nut and carry
her off. When the Giant returned he saw that Iduna was
gone, and put on his eagle-skin to pursue. The Gods were
looking out, and they saw the eagle flying after Loki
and gaining upon him. They feared lest they should lose
Iduna again, perhaps for ever, and they made a plan
quickly to keep out the eagle. They piled up chips of
wood outside Asgard, and stood ready beside them with
torches. At the moment when Loki fluttered down
within the wall they lit the fire. The flames mounted
up as if they were glad to attack the foe of Iduna and
youth. They burnt his wings. He tried to turn, but
in vain ; and had to come to the ground inside the wall
of Asgard. There the Gods set upon him and slew him
gladly. They welcomed back Iduna yet more gladly.

'When Thiazzi's daughter, Skadi, got news of her
father's death, she set out to Asgard to avenge it. She
had eaten of Iduna's apples and she was bold and strong.
But the Gods met her with signs of peace, saying
that they were willing to pay for the death of Thiazzi.
Skadi made her own terms. She said that she must
have a husband from Asgard and be made to laugh.
The Gods accepted these terms, but asked that when
Skadi was choosing her husband she should only see the
feet of the Gods. She was quite willing, and when the
Gods were all ranged before her, hidden from the feet
upwards, she chose the feet which she believed to be
Balder's. But they were Niord's, and Niord became
her husband. It was no easy thing to make her laugh.
Many tricks were tried, but in vain. Then Loki undertook to do it. He worked hard and long, and never had
he been more clever ; he was not still a moment, and
was continually inventing some ridiculous position or
expression ; the sweat poured off him for the first time

in his life : but Thiazzi's daughter did not smile. At last Loki gave up with a face as sad as Skadi's, and full of shame at the antics which seemed absurd when they had no effect. But this sad hang-dog look of her enemy, the treacherous Loki, so delighted her that she burst out laughing, and as this made Loki look more foolish than ever she continued to laugh. How she lived after her marriage with Niord you already know.'

' But if Iduna's apples keep the Gods always young, will they live for ever ? ' asked Gangler.

' Until Ragnarok,' said Har, with a sad voice.

' Tell me about Ragnarok,' said Gangler.

' First,' said Har, ' the Fimbul-winter will come, and men will think it is an ordinary winter. But it will go on and on, and men will forget about summer except when they read the books of the poets. The sun will not be seen or felt. The snow shall drive from all the four quarters with great winds. The frost shall be heavy, and it shall last for the length of three winters. There shall be wars all over the world, and men shall fight with their fathers and their brothers.

' Then the wolf shall swallow the sun, and his brother shall swallow the moon. The stars shall disappear from the sky. The earth shall quake, and the rocks be loosened and the trees fall. The Dwarfs shall swarm out of their caves and know not what to do. Goldcomb, the cock, shall crow again and again to rouse the Gods. Down in Hell the cock Sooty-red shall crow to the hosts of Hell. The Midgard serpent shall lash with his tail and make the sea brim over on to the land. On these waters the ship Naglfar will float with the Giant Rim to steer it. Garm, the hell-hound, shall bay fiercely before the cavern : Fenrir, the wolf-son of Loki, shall break loose from the rocks, and rage over the earth with his mouth gaping, the upper jaw touching heaven, the lower jaw on the earth, and fire blazing from his eyes and nostrils. The Midgard serpent shall join him and crawl over the earth, spouting poison.

' Heaven shall crack with a burning greater than any sunset, and through the opening the sons of Muspell shall come riding. Surtur leads them with a sword brighter than the sun.

' Old Heimdall shall sound his long horn. But nevertheless they shall cross the bridge Bifrost. Surtur and the sons of Muspell shall prance on it. Loki shall break loose and join them, with Fenrir and the Midgard serpent, his sons, and the Giant Rim. Bifrost shall break in pieces, but the host shall be safe, and march to the battle-field called Vigrid. There they shall range themselves, the shining sons of Muspell standing apart in their brightness.

' Far off the Gods shall hear old Heimdall blowing his horn, and Garm the hell-hound barking alone on his chain. Then one of them shall remember what it means and say the word " Ragnarok ". They shall gather together. Odin shall ride down again to Mimir at the brook-side, and ask for his advice. Yggdrasil shall tremble like a young tree. Odin with his golden helmet shall lead out the Gods and the warriors from the five hundred and forty doors of Valhalla. They shall march to the battle-field. Odin shall fight with Fenrir. Thor shall be next to him, but shall be powerless to help him because he has to fight again with the Midgard serpent. Frey without his sword shall have Surtur against him, and he shall die. The dog Garm shall break his chain and join in the battle. He and Tyr shall wrestle and both shall fall, never to rise again. Thor gives the Midgard serpent its death-blow, but he cannot get away fast enough from its dying poison, and he is choked to death. Fenrir swallows Odin, but Vidar rushes up and sets his foot on the lower jaw of the wolf and catches the upper jaw in both his hands, slaying the slayer. Heimdall shall throw away his trumpet and join the battle. Loki shall be his adversary, and both shall perish of their wounds.

' Now the mob from Hell shall sweep darkening over the earth. But Surtur shall flood the earth with a sea and a tempest of fire, and shall burn it and all that is upon it. There shall be nothing but smoke and fire.'

' Yet,' said Gangler, ' what will happen then when the whole world is burnt, and all the Gods dead, and all the host of Valhalla and all mankind, for you have already said that every man shall live in one place or another through all the ages ? '

Then said Thridi :

' There shall be many good abodes and many evil. The best that shall then be is Gimli, which is in heaven. There will be plenty of good drink for lovers of it in the hall named Brimir. Another good hall is Sindri, which is built of red gold on the hills of the moon. These halls are for people who live rightly.

' But in Nastrond there is a foul great hall with doors opening northward. Its walls are a wickerwork of serpents, and all the heads of the serpents are turned inwards and keep spirting venom into the house. This venom runs down in rivers where murderers and liars have to stand.

' It is worse in Vergelmir, where the snake Nidhogg feeds on the living bodies of the worst of sinners.'

' Will there be any Gods alive ? ' asked Gangler.

And Har replied :

' Earth shall rise up out of the sea, beautiful and green, and bear a harvest without sowing. Vidar and Vali, as thou knowest, will be alive, and they shall dwell in Ida-field where Asgard used to be. Modi and Magni, the sons of Thor, shall come there, bringing Miolnir, the hammer. Balder and Hod also shall leave Hell and live in Ida-field. They will talk together more than once about what they have seen and done and suffered in former times, and about Fenrir and the Midgard serpent. And in the grass they shall find the golden tablets of the Gods.

' In the wood of Hodmimir a woman named Lif, and a man named Lifthrasir, shall remain alive, feeding on the dew of morning. Their children shall cover the earth.

' Before she is devoured the sun shall have a daughter lovelier than herself, who shall shine in her course over the sky as the sun does now.

' But if you wish to ask more questions,' said Har, ' I know not where you will find any one to answer you, for I have never heard any one go beyond this point in the history of the world. May you profit by what you have heard.'

Gangler was about to ask, ' And who, then, are ye ? are ye Odin and Thor and Frey or some other Gods ? ' He wanted also to ask where Iduna was. But before he could speak he heard a crash, so that he thought Ragnarok had come, and he was afraid. At first he could see nothing. He looked in vain for Har, Jafnhar, and Thridi. There was not even a hall. He took a few steps and saw no warriors at feast or play or fight, and no man tossing up seven swords and catching them. He saw instead the dead grass of the hill-side very pale in the frosty early evening, and his horse standing by. Then he set out upon his way, and came home and told all that he could remember of what he had heard from those three kings, or gods.

THE VOLSUNGS

I

THE STORY OF SIGMUND

VOLSUNG was a king of the Huns, like his father and grandfather before him. But his grandfather, Sigi, was an outlaw before he was a king. He had gone out hunting with one of his neighbour's thralls, named Bredi; and because the man killed the most deer, Sigi slew him and buried him in a snow-drift. The tale Sigi told was that Bredi had left him and never returned. But the body was found, and Sigi was made an outlaw for his crime. So he left his native country with a band of his father's men.

As an outlaw Sigi had good luck. He and his men took to the trade of fighting for one king or another who was at war, and at last he grew more powerful than any of the kings and had more land. He became King of the Huns, and his queen bore him a son fit to be king after him. When he was a very old man his enemies, and chiefly his wife's brothers, set upon him, slaying him and many of his party. Rerir, his son, escaped almost alone. He recovered the kingdom; he slew his father's murderers; he became a great king and ruled long and gloriously. His sorrow was that he had no children. Not until a little before his death did he know that his queen was at last to bear a child. They had prayed hard to the Gods for a son, but in vain. At last Odin heard the prayer, and Freya came to the

queen and gave her an apple which she bade her take
to the king. She flew to him in the likeness of a crow,
and let the apple fall in his lap. He took it home to
share it with his queen, and soon after this they knew
that their prayer was going to be answered. Rerir died
before he could behold his son. The queen also had to
die before her child could be born ; for so huge was he
that either he or his mother must die, and by her own
choice she died. They called the boy Volsung.

Volsung grew fast in strength and stature, being always
much bigger than other men, as he was born bigger than
they. He ruled Hunland like his father. He was
victorious. He built a royal hall which had a tall oak-
tree standing alive in the midst of it, covering the roof
with its leaves ; and the trunk was called Branstock.
For his wife he took a Giant's daughter, who bore him
ten sons. Of these ten the eldest and mightiest was
Sigmund ; he and Signy, his twin sister, were the best
of Volsung's children, and Sigmund became the father
of a race of heroes.

Signy was sought as a wife by King Siggeir of Gothland, who came himself to the oak-tree hall to ask for
her. She looked at him and did not like him ; she felt
a strong wish not to live with Siggeir and be in his
power in a strange land. Nevertheless, she said that
she would obey her father, and as he liked Siggeir a
marriage was arranged.

Volsung prepared a feast worthy of rich kings and
strong warriors in his oak-tree hall ; Signy was wedded
to Siggeir ; and all sat down to eat and to drink and
to talk and to laugh and to sing and to quarrel. While
they were gathered round the fires in the evening a tall,
one-eyed man, ancient but mighty, neither a Hun nor
a Goth, and bigger than any one in Hunland or Goth-

land, entered the hall unexpected. He was barefooted, with tight linen breeches, a spotted cloak, and a slouched hat. Carrying a sword, he walked up to the Branstock, which he struck with the sword so that it entered into the wood right up to the hilt.

' Whoever shall draw this sword out of the oak,' he said, in a voice worthy of his age and stature, ' shall have it as my gift, and, whoever the man is, he never had a better sword.'

With that the tall man went out of the hall, and was seen no more either by the feasters or by those on the roads.

Kings, nobles, and warriors tried in turn to pull out the sword. None of them could move it. Lastly Sigmund tried, and he drew it as if it had been in a scabbard. Every one saw that it was a good sword, and Siggeir offered thrice its weight in gold for it. But Sigmund said :

' The gold is thine, Siggeir, by right : so also is the sword mine, and I will hold it.'

Siggeir thought that he spoke in scorn ; he held his tongue, and began to think how he might pay Sigmund back for his scorn. Next morning he told King Volsung that he would go back to Gothland that day, giving as his excuse that the weather was fair and the sea smooth, and that if they let this fine day go by they might lose a score of days after it by storm. As it was plain that Siggeir did not wish to remain at the feast, Volsung and his sons did not argue with him. They would not listen to Signy's words :

' I wish I had not to go away with Siggeir. I know that some great misfortune will befall us, and not me only, if I go with him.'

' Daughter,' said Volsung, ' Siggeir has done nothing

that can be blamed. If we take back thy promise to him he will reward us with evil.'

So Signy left home with a hard face, after Siggeir had invited Volsung and his sons to Gothland for a return visit.

In three months' time Volsung and his sons landed on the Gothic shore out of their three ships. Signy was waiting for them in the darkness. Those three months had made her not merely a queen but a fierce-hearted woman, crafty and bold. She came to tell her father that Siggeir was treacherous; he was getting ready for them not feasts but battles; his army was too big for them to resist. Her advice was that they should slip back to gather a strong enough host. Volsung would not. ' In those six years before I was born,' he said, ' I vowed that I would never fly from steel or fire. I am old and have not broken the vow, nor will I in the little time between this and the day when I must die. I must die, yet I can die but once. Until the last day I shall choose to live as a man ought to do, lest afterwards I should have no choice.'

Signy wept, for she had not shed a tear since she left home, but Volsung only said :

' Go back to thy husband and stay with him, whatever happens to us.'

Volsung and his sons and their men were stirring early in the morning, ready for Siggeir. Siggeir was ready for them; his army fell upon them in the first light of day. No man could resist Volsung and his ten sons. Like reapers they cut their way through Siggeir's army and back again, eight times. But Volsung was an old man, and he fell; and as a broad field of corn tires the strongest reapers in the end, so that huge army tired the sons of Volsung. All were taken prisoners.

When Signy knew that her brothers were to die she
went to King Siggeir. ' Do not kill my brothers at once,'
she said, ' spare them a little longer, if it be only in the
stocks, that I may see them and they me.'

' Thou must be mad,' he said, ' to make their death
worse by putting it off. But have thy way. I care not
how much thou addest to their sufferings, and die they
shall at the end and not live.'

The way Siggeir kept his promise was to have the
ten brothers taken far out into a wood, there to be laid
in a row with their legs covered by a huge beam, so
that they could not escape. There they lay all day.
At night a great she-wolf out of the forest killed one
of the brothers and devoured him. Signy was kept a
prisoner by the king, and could not go to her brothers.
But she sent a messenger to bring tidings of them, and
he told her that the she-wolf had eaten one. Day after
day he brought no other tidings than this : that in the
night the she-wolf had eaten one of her brothers. At
length only Sigmund was left alive. When Signy
heard it she sent the messenger swiftly back again with
some honey, which he was to smear over Sigmund's
face. In the night came the wolf, intending to kill and
eat Sigmund. He lay perfectly still. First, the wolf
licked the honey clean off his face. When there was
no more to be had, she thrust her tongue into his mouth
to seek for more. If she found any honey she could not
swallow it; for Sigmund took firm hold of her tongue with
his teeth. She pulled with all her might without loosening his grip, and thus at last, by working his legs about,
Sigmund contrived that she set him free from the beam.
But he did not let go of her tongue ; it was the wolf
that let go of it and soon afterwards died.

When Signy heard of Sigmund's escape, and Siggeir

supposed that he also had been eaten by the wolf, she went out into the woods to see her brother where he was living wild and alone. By her advice he made a house underground in the wood, to dwell in until they could plan some certain revenge. From time to time Signy sent him whatever he had need of.

Thus ten years passed. Signy and Siggeir had two sons, and the first-born was ten years old. Now Signy sent this elder boy to Sigmund for a help and a companion. Sigmund gave him a good welcome at evening in his dark house. The first work that he gave the boy was to get ready the bread for baking while he himself fetched wood for the fire. The boy found something in the meal-bag besides meal, something alive, which frightened him though he did not see what it was, and he did nothing but tie up the neck of the bag as tightly as possible. Sigmund came home and found nothing done. ' There was something wriggling in the bag,' said the boy, ' but I kept it safe for you.' By this Sigmund knew that he was more Siggeir's child than Signy's. His mother had no pity on him. ' Kill him,' she said, on hearing the tale. ' What use is he ? ' And Sigmund killed the boy.

A year later the younger boy came to Sigmund. He also was a coward, and he was killed like his brother, by the advice of Signy.

Sigmund dwelt alone in his house under the ground, living on memories of the oak-tree hall and on hopes of revenge, and keeping bright the sword that fed both his memories and his hopes.

After that Signy bore another son, bigger and stronger than his brothers had been. His name was Sinfiotli, and his mother taught him to hate King Siggeir and to love her brother, Sigmund. All his boasting was of his hero forefathers; all his ambition was to be like them. When his mother stitched gloves on to his hands in such a way that the skin came off with the gloves, he only said : ' That would have been nothing to Volsung, my grandfather.'

In due time Sinfiotli went to Sigmund's house in the woods. He, too, was left to make the bread. He kneaded up the meal with both hands, never troubling about what was mixed up with it except to make sure by his lusty kneading that it was less alive at last than at first. Sigmund came home with the firewood as he was finishing. ' Was the meal right ? ' he asked. ' Yes,' said the boy ; ' but there was something alive in it when I began. I thought that was perhaps your woodland way.'

Sigmund laughed : ' Thou art a good boy, Sinfiotli, but I will keep this bread for myself. What thou kneaded up in it was a deadly snake. At least, it would be deadly to thee, though not to me.' At this the boy cried because his stomach would not stand poison like Sigmund's.

Now that he had a good companion Sigmund lived less in his earth house. He and Sinfiotli ranged together in the woods, setting upon small bands of travellers and killing them for the sake of their gold and weapons. For a time they took the form of wolves, the fiercest wolves ever known in the forest. Sinfiotli was as fearless as Sigmund and had less pity, which made Sigmund think that the boy had the bravery of Volsung but the fell nature of Siggeir. The boy did not learn from Sigmund to love King Siggeir. Often he talked of avenging the death of Volsung and Volsung's nine sons, and the captivity of his own mother, Signy; he spoke of the day when they would be the death of King Siggeir.

This life trained Sinfiotli for the great revenge. He grew to be the equal of Sigmund in strength and cunning, though each was so powerful that when either one did a deed by himself no one who saw it would believe that the other could do as much. Their plan was to lie in wait for King Siggeir among some tuns of ale standing in the porch of the hall. They got there unseen of any one save Signy. As they were crouching in the dark a golden ball rolled up to their feet, and after it came running the two little princes who were playing with it. The two men were motionless, and at first the children were delighted to see the swords and the mail-coats. Then one of them caught sight of Sinfiotli's eyes and teeth; he could not take his eyes off the fierce face; he stood perfectly still and stared. But the other child, seeing the look of horror on his brother's face, ran up the hall to his father. Signy guessed what had happened. Before Siggeir could understand the boy's story, she rose and went swiftly out to the porch. 'The child has betrayed ye,' she whispered as she was passing, 'kill him and be ready.' Sigmund would not hurt the child, but Sinfiotli slew him and cast the body out of his way.

In another moment a cry was raised. Siggeir was bidding his men to arm and search the porch. They swarmed out, but the two men cut down all who approached them. Others now attacked from the outside, rushing on them in such numbers that swords had no room to swing. In this crush Sigmund and Sinfiotli were no better than sheep, and like sheep they were taken and bound. They were doomed to be buried alive.

A burial-place was made ready for them in the morning. It was a plot of land surrounded by a ring of turf and stones, and divided into two parts by one huge stone

standing on its edge like a wall. In one half they put
Sinfiotli; and in the other, Sigmund. Then men began
to cover up the tomb with big stones and turf. In this
way the two would have been starved to death in their
separate graves. But Signy had persuaded a man to
throw in with the turf an armful of straw in which she
had hidden a piece of swine's flesh and Sigmund's sword
sticking in it. This straw fell into Sinfiotli's half. When
all was still and the burial-mound complete, and ready
to be grown over with grass and last a thousand years,
Sinfiotli told Sigmund the news. They were lighter-
hearted. Sinfiotli thrust the sword through the stone;
Sigmund caught the point and drew it towards him.
Sigmund pushing and Sinfiotli pulling, and then Sinfiotli pushing and Sigmund pulling, they used the sword
like a two-handed saw until they had sawed through
the stone. They heaved over one half of the stone,
and then Sinfiotli went through to Sigmund. They
now took it in turns to work at one part of their
grave until they had cut a way right through and let
themselves out.

With the sword sharpened they walked swiftly to
Siggeir's hall. Every one slept there, weary with
fighting, except the few that had not yet died of their
wounds. These wounded men cried out to warn King
Siggeir that Sigmund and Sinfiotli were back again,
but the king and the others were too well used to the
cries of the wounded to be awakened by them. The two
were piling up dry wood in the hall, taking no more
notice of the wounded men than their sleeping companions did. Having failed to waken the others, the
wounded were saving themselves by crawling out.
When the pile was tall enough Sigmund set fire to it.
The flames leapt up to the roof in their first glad-

ness, kindling the thatch before settling down to burn steadily in the heart of the pile. The kindly warmth pleased the sleepers until the smoke began to stifle them. Then there was a shouting and a running to and fro, and the wounded men crawled away more swiftly out in the dark. In the hall some ran on to the swords of Sigmund and Sinfiotli in trying to escape the flames; some ran away from the swords into the flames; others died from the fall of the flaming roof. Siggeir had only been awakened by Sigmund calling out to Signy to come out and save herself. The king was in a greater hurry than his queen, yet he was slow to face his enemies' flames or weapons. At his side, Signy's face was as fierce as fire or sword. 'This is my work, King Siggeir,' she said. 'Now thou art paid for the honour thou didst me when thou madest me queen of the Goths. Volsung also is partly paid for thy treachery when thou didst slay him and my brothers, thine invited guests. I also am partly paid for these years with thee, for I think that thou wilt die before me, and after that there is no pleasure left that I desire except death.' With these words she walked through the fire to kiss her brother and her son and back again to Siggeir's side, where she died a little after him.

Sigmund gladly sailed with Sinfiotli from Gothland to his own country. They drove out the usurper from Volsung's place; they made the kingdom stronger than ever; and Sigmund took a wife, named Borghild. Two sons, Helgi and Hamond, were born to Sigmund. At the birth of the elder the Norns came to the cradle to prophesy. Helgi was to be a most famous king, they said; and at the age of fifteen he was fit for the wars like any other man; he was wise also and well beloved.

Sinfiotli cared less for fighting with the king's armies than for rapid forays with his chosen men, to plunder and fight. In one of these he caught sight of Swintha, Queen of the Varns, and loved her. But he had to fight another lover before he could win her. Sinfiotli was the victor and he won Queen Swintha. The dead man, as it fell out, was Borghild's brother. When Sinfiotli returned home he told Sigmund this news, and Sigmund told it to the queen. Borghild was very angry, and wished Sigmund to send Sinfiotli out of the land; but he would not. The queen, therefore, pretended to be satisfied with a large fine in gold for her brother's life. At the funeral feast she smiled more on Sinfiotli than any one. Most of all she smiled in offering him a horn of mead, saying, ' Drink, Sinfiotli.'

Sinfiotli looked into the horn and said :

' O Queen, the mere sight of this drink quenches my thirst, so good is it.'

He held it out for Borghild to take back, but Sigmund took it instead and drank it, for he could drink anything. This angered the queen. ' Why,' said she to Sinfiotli, ' why do other men drink thine ale for thee ? '

' I think,' was his answer, ' that only Sigmund could drink such ale, and I am sure that none but he would willingly do so.'

Yet Borghild offered him another horn, saying, ' Drink this, Sinfiotli.'

Again Sigmund drained the horn instead of Sinfiotli.

The third time the queen said to Sinfiotli, laughing :

' Drink this, if thou art a Volsung.'

He took the horn, but he said right out :

' This drink is poison, O Queen.'

Then Sigmund spoke. He was drunk, and he knew not what would come of his words :

' Drink, Sinfiotli, and strain out the poison with thy lips.'

But this could not be done, and when Sinfiotli had drained the horn he fell dead.

Sigmund looked at Borghild, yet finished the horn he was drinking. After that he did not look at her again. He bent down and picked up Sinfiotli and carried him out of the hall, bidding men not to follow. He traversed a dark wood, and at the far end of it came to a long firth of sea. By the shore lay a small boat ; by the boat stood a barefooted tall man in a cloak, old but mighty. ' Shall I take him over ? ' said the tall old man. ' Yes,' said Sigmund, and he waded into the water and laid the body of Sinfiotli in the boat. Sigmund would have entered also, but there was no room except for the ferryman. He turned round then to see if the ferryman was coming, but he had vanished. Coming ashore, he looked far up the firth and far out to the sea in vain. When he stepped again towards the boat he saw that it was gone.

So Sigmund returned home. He drove out Queen Borghild, and for some time he lived alone. Then he felt a wish to take Hiordis, daughter of King Eylimi, for a wife. She was beautiful and wise, and her father was a great king. Sigmund made a journey to see King Eylimi. At the same time another king, Lyngi, the son of King Hunding, journeyed there on the same errand. King Eylimi was much perplexed, and therefore he left his daughter Hiordis to choose for herself between the two kings. Her choice fell upon Sigmund. He stayed for the wedding, but Lyngi did not. On his way home again with his bride he was set upon by Lyngi and a very great host. Sigmund was irresistible as of old, and many a sad man ended his troubles, and many a joyous one his joy, at the point of Sigmund's sword. Where Sigmund was not, there his men failed before the men of King Lyngi. The enemy fled from Sigmund, but they overwhelmed his men. At last one was found to stand up to Sigmund, a tall, one-eyed old man in a blue cloak, wearing a slouched hat. He came steadily towards Sigmund with a spear in his hand. Fiercely Sigmund struck at him, but the sword hit only the spear and broke in two; and the old man vanished. Sigmund had no more good fortune. He fought only because he knew not how to run away or what good could come of it. At last he fell deeply wounded, with a multitude of his men and King Eylimi, father of Hiordis. Hiordis herself was hiding in the woods, and King Lyngi could not find her. After dark she stole out and came upon Sigmund still alive on the battle-field. She would have healed his wounds, but he refused, because the sword which he had taken from the Branstock was broken and he knew that Odin had given the sign for his death. She begged him to stay to avenge her father's death. ' Another will do that,' said he ; ' thou wilt bear a child, and it will be a man child. Look well after him, for he will be worthy of it. Keep the halves of my sword, and in time he will use it. His name will endure for ever. Now let me die.' And Hiordis sat by him until he was dead, and when she had buried him she went away, carrying the pieces of Sigmund's sword.

II

THE STORY OF HELGI

ONE son of Sigmund was alive when the king met his death. That was Helgi, Borghild's child, who had yet to fulfil the prophecy of the Norns. They had come at his birth to forecast his life. In the silence of the moon-light they twisted the strands of fate for him far and wide over the earth. One of them, Neri's sister, fastening a strand in the North, prayed that it might hold for ever. All said that he would be called the best of princes and the most famous of warrior kings. One said that he would be unfortunate.

At the edge of the wood near the king's hall two ravens sat high on an oak as the day was beginning to break. They were so starved that they could hardly fly, though their bodies had become no heavier than doves, and they sat and talked of nothing but the new Volsung's birth. For it gave them hope of feasting before many years.

' I know something,' said one. ' A son was born to Sigmund this night. His armour is gleaming and his eyes are glittering this moment in the light of dawn. He is a friend of wolves and of ravens. Let us be of good cheer.'

' Let us be patient,' said the other.

The beauty and shapeliness of the child pleased every one, the men as much as the women, and they said :

' Now shall good seasons come among men.'

Sigmund hastened from the battle-field home, bringing a leek for his beautiful child for a sign of kingship. He gave him the name of Helgi. He made him gifts at once of halls and lands called Ringstead, Sunfell, Snowfell, Sigarsfell, Ringhaven, Hightown, and Heavening. He gave him a sword with a handle inwrought by the best workmen.

When Sigmund married Hiordis, Helgi was living with Hagal, his foster-father. After the fatal battle with Lyngi, where Sigmund died, Hagal saved Helgi, and cunningly sent him to live in the hall of King Hunding, Lyngi's father. There he stayed unsuspected until his size might have betrayed him as Sigmund's son. Then he slipped away again to Hagal. From Hagal's house he sent a message to Hunding, telling him that it was not Hagal's own son that he had been protecting, as he thought, but a wolf-cub, Sigmund's son, who knew that Hunding had been his father's enemy and would not forget it. Hunding sent men to look for Helgi. The lad was disguised as a bondmaid grinding corn. His fierce eyes betrayed him to one of the searchers, who said to himself:

'Hagal's bondmaid has fierce eyes, no slave-born maid is she who is grinding the corn. No maid either, but a youth, and a king's son, methinks. The grip of a sword would fit those hands better than a mill-handle. . . .'

The rattling of the mill under those strong hands scared the man, and he exclaimed: 'No, no! my girl, I said nothing.' Helgi said to him, smiling:

'It is no wonder the mill rattles as I turn it. I am one of the cloud-riders. I am a sister of Sigar and Hogni, and before Helgi captured me I fought as warriors do, although a maiden. That is why my eyes are a little wild.'

The fellow was glad to go, and to get out of reach of those eyes and those hands. He did not long save his life. Helgi and his step-father gathered Sigmund's friends together and set upon Hunding. They routed his army, and Helgi himself slew the king. Hunding's sons asked Helgi for gold to atone for their father's death. He refused them even so much as a ring. He answered them with spears in the battle of Lowefell. Most of them he slew, and scattered the others before he sat down at the foot of the Eagle-rock to rest. The sun was now burning through the dark clouds of the afternoon, and Helgi watched the white fire. He watched until he saw coming out of it, or from the clouds beyond, a troop of what seemed to be women, but riding high in the field of heaven. They were armed like warriors with glittering spears, and their helmets and coats of mail were blood-stained. They were Valkyries, as Helgi knew before they descended one by one to the earth in front of him, shining and beautiful and wild. All he could say to them was :

' Valkyries, will ye feast with me to-night ? '

But they plucked their bowstrings, and the leader of them answered him straight from the saddle :

' It is not to drink ale under a roof with you, Helgi, that we have ridden from yonder. No. This is what is the matter. My father Hogni has promised me as a bride for King Hodbrord, Granmar's grim son. I care no more for Hodbrord than a cat; but it was no good for me to say so. In a few days he will come to fetch me away, unless thou wilt challenge him to battle and deliver me out of his hand.'

With these words she leapt from her horse and kissed Helgi upon the mouth, for she had loved him before ever he had seen her.

' If I live, maiden,' said Helgi, ' there shall be a rattle of blades before Hodbrord carries thee away.'

Then the maiden, whose name was Sigrun, smiled on
him and galloped away with the others upon the wild
wind over the sea.

Helgi roused himself from his seat beneath the Eagle-
rock. He sent messengers to go swiftly by land and sea
to gather an army, promising the warriors and their sons
more gold than ever they had before. Helgi went to
Brandey harbour to wait for the ships and the land hosts.
It was a great army when all were together. They went
aboard and hoisted the sails at dawn. The plashing of
oars mingled with the clanging of the Vikings' shields
at the sides of the ships; but the noise of the sea
drowned the other noises. Hardly could the ships
have lived' among these ever-changing hills of water
had not Sigrun ridden upon the winds above them,
to give them more courage and more cunning than
ever before. With her help they got safely to Hodbrord's
land, and the enemy, catching sight of them, wondered
who was the king with the golden standard flying at the
bows of his ship. They knew at least that the fleet came
for battle. For they saw no shield of peace, but a dreadful
halo of war about the Vikings.

One of Helgi's men rose up and taunted one of
Hodbrord's men who was watching them land:

'When you are feeding the pigs this evening, my man,
do not forget to tell people that the Wolfings are here
in a fighting mood. Tell Hodbrord that here he will
find Helgi the king, one who has been a careful feeder
of eagles and ravens while you have been flirting with
slave-girls at the corn-mills.'

'Take care,' said Hodbrord's man, 'take care you are
not feeding ravens with your own carcass before I feed
the pigs.'

'It will not be you that gives me to the ravens. You

look fit for skipping about after goats on the rocks, with
a hazel stick for a sword.'

'Who was your king's father? One that was once
a wolf and ate wolf's meat and lived in wolves' houses
and heard the wolves' songs.'

'As for you, you were a witch-hag, and you have
had a bit in your mouth and a bridle, and what is more,
I have ridden you up hill and down dale myself, you . . .'

But Helgi interrupted the wrangling.

'It would be better,' said he impatiently, 'to fight
and gladden the eagle than to waste good words. They
are my enemies, but they are brave men, and it does us
no credit to make them out fools or cowards.'

Two of Hodbrord's men now rode away. Their
horses, Sweepwood and Swaywood, ran with all speed
through many dark glens and misty hollows to Sunham,
where Hodbrord met them at the gate of his court.
'Why are ye flushed with anger?' he asked them.

'The Wolfings,' they answered, 'are landing. We
saw their dark sea-stags touch our shore. Fifteen
battalions are landing, and there are seven thousand
more farther down the coast. Helgi will not wait.'

Hodbrord said only :

'Bridle the fleetest horses! Mount and ride through
Mirkwood and over Sparin's Heath and gather a great
army! Let no man keep away who can wield a sword!
Call Hogni and the sons of Ring, Atli, Yngwi, Alf the
Old! They are eager for war.'

At the Wolf-rock the two armies met. Men hewed
and stabbed and thrust. There was a shouting and
a grunting and a groaning, as they rushed to and fro
or slowly pushed back their enemies or gave way before
them. All men were skilled in this trade, and harder
they toiled at it than ever carpenter, shoemaker, or

ploughman. Helgi laboured hard like one who did not
like the way men were made and was striving to shape
them different. Yet when he had shaped one by cutting
off a head or shortening his legs he went on to another
and forgot about the first. He slew all who came against
him. In the air the Valkyries swept to and fro watching
the fight. Sometimes Sigrun called to him : ' Helgi !
Helgi ! ' and his strength doubled. And when Hogni
lay dead, and there was no more enemy, she hailed him
as victor, king, and her own lord. Nor did she spare to
visit Hodbrord where he lay dying, and to say :

' Sigrun from Sevafell shall never rest, O King
Hodbrord, in thy arms. Thy life is over, and the whole
race of Granmar is at an end.'

Then she rode again to Helgi, and alighted at his side
and kissed him.

' Sigrun,' he said to her, ' thou hast been as a war-
goddess to me to-day. And yet, fairy, thou canst not
have everything as thou wouldst wish. Much thou hast
done. Something has Fate done also ; for, alas ! I have
been the slayer of many men of thy kin, thy father,
Hogni, and thy brothers all but one. One of those that
died was the fiercest enemy that ever I had, for he
fought after his head was off. This was none of thy
work, and would that it had not been mine ! '

Said Sigrun :

' Truly should I be glad if some of those who are dead
were alive, yet gladly will I now shelter me in thine arms,
O Helgi.'

So Helgi married Sigrun, and they lived together
happily. Helgi was still victorious over men and Giants.
Nor did Sigrun forget how to ride in the air and aid his
conquests. When he sailed over the sea against Hati
the Giant she guarded the fleet from the sorcery of

Rimegerd, the Giant's daughter. He slew the Giant, and having got his army safely on board ship again the fleet lay moored for the night under the cliffs. Only Atli, the warder of Helgi, was awake, keeping watch on deck, when Rimegerd appeared above on the cliffs and called to him :

'Who is the lord of this fleet ? You come boastfully, as if you were safe. Tell me the name of your king ! '

'Our king,' said Atli, ' is our king, if you want to know. But *you* can do him no harm. Ogresses cannot hurt him.'

'And who are you ? '

'My name is Atli. Some call me Ate, and perhaps I shall prove hateful to you if you try any of your ogress tricks. Many a night-rider have I slain when I have been in the wave-washed bows of our ship. And who are you ? '

'I am Rimegerd, Hati's daughter.'

'I know. You were swimming before Helgi's ships to wreck them, but you had no luck, Rimegerd.'

'No. That was not me, but my mother. It was I that drowned the sons of Lodvar in the deep, if you can remember such little things.'

Rimegerd laughed at him. She was trying hard to lure him from the ship with her talk. But he always found words for an answer. Then she wakened Helgi himself with shouting :

'Get up, Helgi ! and pay me for the slaughter of my poor dear father, Hati. Or if you will come and wed me I will let you off the payment.'

'Ogresses should have ogres, Rimegerd,' said Helgi.

'Oh ! I know your heart, Helgi. You would rather have her that was watching last night over the haven.

Without Sigrun you would never have landed, and without Sigrun you would not be here to-night.'

'Ogresses know their betters. Tell me, Rimegerd—and if you do I will pay you what Hati was worth—how many of the Valkyries were there in the air ? Or was it only one ? '

'One rode before the others dressed in white, with a helmet. But there were three times nine altogether. Their steeds shook dew from their manes into the valleys and hail on to the hill-tops as they reared on the wind. I hate them all.'

Rimegerd had stayed too long talking. Never would she leave the edge of the cliff now that the sun was up, and Atli laughed loudly at her in triumph :

'Rimegerd ! Rimegerd ! look eastward. The ships are safe now from Rimegerd, for it is day. It is day, Rimegerd ! and day is not for ogresses. You have talked too long. You are stone now instead of ogre-flesh. Now you will be some good to men. You shall stand as a harbour-mark for sailors, and also you shall make them laugh for many a year. Stone is better than ogre-flesh except for ogres, Rimegerd.'

Thus Helgi came safely back to Sigrun. In their happiness they were forgetting that one son of Hogni, called Day, was still alive. Day had nothing to make him forget Helgi. He prayed to Odin for help in avenging his father's death, and he dwelt in the forest, looking for a chance to strike at his enemy. At last an hour came when Day found Helgi alone in the forest. Day had a spear from Odin with which he could not miss Helgi's heart, and Helgi died. Day himself brought the bad news to Sigrun :

'Sorry am I for thee, my sister, that I have slain him who was the best of earthly princes and dearer to thee

than any among the living or the dead. But I loved
him not, any more than he loved our father and our
brothers, and as he slew them so I have slain him.'

Sigrun answered him only with cursing :

' May the ship thou art in never sail, even with a fair
wind aft ! May the horse thou ridest never run, though
thy foemen are following after thy life ! May the sword
thou drawest never bite any except thyself ! Would
that thou wert an outlaw solitary in the woods with
no meat but carrion, miserably envying the dead but
afraid to die ! '

' Sister, this is folly to curse a brother. Besides, it
was Odin that did the harm. He made the strife
between us. Yet I will give thee half of my land to make
up for the wrong I have done.'

She took no heed of his words, for she was thinking :

' Never again shall I sit happy at Sevafell, or have joy
at morn or evening ; for never again shall I see the
sunlight flash on my lord's company, never see his war-
horse with the gold bit bearing home my king, never
welcome him again. Helgi was as a wolf to his foemen,
and they were as goats. There was none like him. He
stood among other kings like an ash among thorns or
as the leading stag among the deer. See him in Odin's
hall ! He calls King Hunding to get ready a bath
for his feet and tie up the hounds and bait the horses.
" Hunding ! " he says, " give the hogs their swill before
thou goest to sleep." Oh Helgi ! Helgi ! '

She was wild with sorrow. Day by day, after they had
buried Helgi under a mound fit for such a king, she sat
expecting to see him again. One day she had waited
until sunset, and she muttered :

' The son of Sigmund would have been here by now
if he was coming from Odin's halls. I have but a faint

hope left now when the eagles are settling on the ash-tree for the night, and the household are thronging to the house of dreams.'

And she left her bondmaid alone by the burial-mound. Suddenly she heard the bondmaid shriek out :

' Is that a phantom I am looking at, or is the Doom of the Powers come ? Sure, dead men cannot ride and prick their steeds with spurs ? . . . Or have ye truly come home at last, as the queen expected ? Look, look ! '

The leading rider answered :

' Thou seest no phantom, but men riding home and using the spur. Sigrun ! Sigrun ! Come out of Sevafell. The burial-mound is opened. I am Helgi come out to see thee, and to ask thee to stanch my wounds. They are bleeding still.'

Sigrun ran towards him, past the bondmaid, who tried to stop her :

' Go not alone to the houses of the Ghosts. It is dark now, and the dead fiends grow stronger with the dark.'

Sigrun could not be stopped. She heard Helgi saying :

' Come and stay the bleeding of my wounds. I must be on the other side of the rainbow before cock-crow.'

She fell upon his neck and kissed him, murmuring loudly :

' I am as glad to see thee as famishing hawks to scent their warm prey or to see the dawn break. I will kiss thee now, my dead king, before thou cast off thy gory mail-coat. O Helgi ! thy hair is thick with hoar-frost ! thy body is drenched with dew ! thy hands are cold and dank ! what can I do ? '

' Sigrun from Sevafell,' he answered, ' through thee am I drenched with this dew. For night after night, O sunbright lady of the South, thou weepest cruel tears ere thou sleepest, and every tear falls bloody, dank, and cold on my breast.'

She went with him into the grave.

'Let us drink together, Sigrun!' said Helgi, 'let us drink costly draughts, though we have no longer love or land. Let no man chant dirges for me though he see the wounds on my breast; for now are maidens, royal ladies, become companions for dead men in graves!'

Sigrun let his head gently down as if on a pillow, and smoothed his hair. He lay still and she stretched herself out beside him. 'Never,' said Helgi, 'was there a greater marvel at Sevafell than for thee to join me in the grave, the dead by the living.'

When she awoke at cock-crow she was drenched with dew and her hair was stiff with hoar-frost, but she saw only the bondmaid and felt only the bondmaid's arms about her, carrying her back into the hall. Then as no other night was like that night, and no day ever gave her to Helgi or Helgi to her, she pined away in weariness and died.

THE STORY OF SIGURD

I

HELGI's more famous brother, Sigurd, was not yet born when his father, Sigmund, died on the battle-field. Hiordis, the queen, had only the unborn child and the two pieces of Sigmund's sword when she went into the woods with one bondmaid to hide; for they saw many ships sailing towards the land. In the wood Hiordis changed dresses with the woman, who was to call herself the queen and Hiordis her bondmaid. But the men in the ships had seen them, and having found them and the treasure which they had hidden, led them on board. Alf, son of King Hialprek of Denmark, was the captain, and as he sat at the tiller he questioned the women. For he saw that she who called herself the bondmaid knew well how to behave in the company of noble men, and he tried to get at the bottom of the mystery. But he learned hardly anything. In Denmark Alf's mother, the queen, soon saw that there was a mystery. She wanted to know why the fairer of the two women had fewer rings and poorer raiment than the other. So she sat down by them, and after getting into talk with them asked the one who called herself Hiordis :

' How can you tell in your country what time it is in the winter nights, when the stars are hidden ? '

' When I was a young girl,' she said, ' I had to be up at the same hour, summer and winter, about the time of sunrise in the middle of May ; and even now I always wake at that hour, though, of course, I do not rise so early.'

' Strange for a king's daughter ! ' laughed the old queen. Then she asked the one who called herself bond-maid the same question, and she answered :

' My father gave me a gold ring that always grows chill on my finger at dawn, and thus I know the time.'

At this the old queen laughed still more.

' There was plenty of gold in that country for a bond-maid to have a ring of it ! But now we have had enough of secrets.'

So they all laughed together and the queen told her son, and he said to Hiordis :

' If thou hadst not hidden this I should have treated thee as I thought thou deservedst; but I shall not hide anything from thee, and especially one thing, that thou shalt be my wife.'

In a little while Hiordis gave birth to Sigmund's child. Looking at the boy's keen eyes, King Hialprek judged that he would make a man without an equal. He was given the name of Sigurd, and he grew up strong and big and of a generous nature ; and his mother married King Alf.

Sigurd spent his boyhood with a foster-father named Regin, one of the Dwarfs who are clever at working with metals. As soon as he saw the boy Regin said :

' The son of Sigmund, a keen warrior, has come to us. He has more courage than many a man, and the grip of a wolf. I will bring him up, and he shall be the mightiest king under the sun.'

Regin taught him many things, such as writing, languages, and chess, which were thought right for the sons of kings. In everything the boy pleased his foster-

father except that he was too contented. Regin asked
him if he knew how much treasure belonged to him
and who had charge of it, and when he answered that
the kings were keeping it for him, asked if he trusted
them completely. ' It is well,' said Sigurd, ' that they
should keep it so long as they know better than I how
to do so.'

At another time Regin asked why it was that he ran
about on foot like any other boy, and not like the son of
a king. ' If I like I can have a horse,' he replied ; ' they
give me whatever I want.' ' Then ask for a horse,'
said Regin ; and Sigurd asked the king for a horse, and
the king bade him choose one for himself and anything
else that he might want. Sigurd was going next day
to look for a horse when he met a tall old man, a stranger,
with a slouched hat and cloak, who asked where he was
going, and he told him. The old man advised him to
drive the herd of horses down into the river, and he
himself would help. The horses entered the river
quickly enough, but all went the shortest way to land,
except one, who swam right across. That one Sigurd
took for his own. It was a grey horse, young, but
strong and big and wild. The old man said : ' Take care
of him. He is one of Sleipnir's sons, and he will turn
out the best horse in this world.' He was given the
name of Grani, which is a name no more to be forgotten
than Sigurd.

Seeing the strength of the lad, Regin planned to use it
for getting a treasure that he knew of. He said : ' Why
should you run about like a churl's son when you might
be getting wealth and honour with it ? I know a treasure
of gold which no king ever saw the like of. It lies not
very far off on Glistenheath, guarded by the dragon
Fafnir, a very famous dragon that men talk much of—

too much, perhaps; but thou, Sigurd, art not his match,
though thou dost come of the race of Volsung and art
Sigmund's son.'

'I dare say,' said Sigurd, 'I am too young to have
all the heart and sense of those heroes, but why shouldest
thou call me coward? Thou dost not *think* me one,
but callest me the name to make me attempt what is
perhaps beyond me.'

'I will tell thee the tale,' Regin answered. 'My
father was a great and rich man, and his name was
Rodmar. He had two sons before me, Fafnir and Otter.
Fafnir was the biggest and grimmest of us : he did little,
but he wanted to own everything near him and to keep
every one else away from it, while he slept in the midst
of his possessions. Otter was the cleverest : he lived
chiefly in the water; he did not like the land, yet he
brought our father great wealth of salmons. One day
he had been fishing under a waterfall, and was falling
asleep over the best part of a salmon that he had
caught, when three Gods came by, Odin, Loki, and
Haenir. He did not escape Loki's eyes. Picking up
a big stone, the God threw it at Otter with all his might,
so that he died. They skinned him, and in the evening
they came to Rodmar's house. They showed Rodmar
the skin. "You have slain my son Otter," said the old
man, "and you shall pay for it according to the law
of this country, which is that you shall fill the skin full
of gold and also cover it altogether with gold." In
the pool by the waterfall where Otter had lived, a Dwarf
named Andwari lived also in the shape of a pike; for
an evil Norn had given him that shape long ago, and con-
demned him to the water. But he still had with him
in the rocks a very great treasure. Loki went to look
for this treasure with a net borrowed from Ran, who

was the wife of Eager, the Sea God. He caught Andwari
and made him give up the gold that he had concealed
in the rocks under water. One ring only did he keep
back, yet Loki knew it and sent him back for it.
Andwari gave him the ring, adding this curse, which
was to go with the ring:

' " This treasure shall be the death of two brothers.
It shall make feuds among eight kings. Nobody shall
have joy of it."

' Loki was not long in filling the skin of Otter with
gold. Covering it was more difficult. For Rodmar tied
the very tip of the tail to a branch so that the heavy
body only just weighed the tip of the nose down to the
ground, and the Gods had to pile up the gold until not
a hair could be seen. To cover the last hairs Loki had
to produce the ring that went with the curse. He did
not forget the curse. " Here is your gold," he said,
" and far too much of it. But there is no luck with it.
It will be the death of you and your sons."

' " You do not like parting with your gold," retorted
Rodmar, " I know very well that you give it without
love. If I had known you were coming this way
with your mischief you would have died instead of
my son."

' " Don't talk now," said Loki, " but wait until you
know as much as I, though you will never know all,
because some of those who will suffer by this curse are
not yet born."

' " You can't frighten me," said Rodmar; " until I die
I shall enjoy the red gold, and I am not afraid of what
may happen after. Be off with you ! "

' But Loki was right. Before long Fafnir slew the old
man for the sake of the treasure. He would let me have
none of it, so I became a smith, and he lies coiled up

all over the gold like the roots of a tree. It is a wondrous
treasure.'

'You have been unlucky,' said Sigurd. 'But if I am
to kill your brother for you, I must have a sword, a good
sword, and then, should I have the strength, you may yet
have your treasure. You are the second brother. Have
you any brothers left besides Fafnir?'

Regin did not answer. He was in a hurry to make
a sword, and he made a bad one, which Sigurd broke
at the first trial. He made a second one that was better,
but not strong enough for Sigurd. 'Are you a liar and
traitor like the rest of your family?' asked Sigurd.
Then he remembered the two pieces of his father's
sword, Gram, which his mother kept in a safe place.
He went to his mother and she gave him the sword,
because his face told her that he would be worthy of it.
He took it at once to Regin, bidding him make a good
sword out of those good pieces. And so he did, and
a fire seemed to burn along the two edges of it as it
was carried out of the forge. Regin said: 'I cannot
make a sword if this is not a good one.' Sigurd said
nothing, but grasped it and struck at the anvil with it.
The good blade cut clean through the anvil without
a hurt. Next Sigurd went down to the river and threw
a lock of wool in, and held the sword so that the water
carried the wool against the edge of the blade. The wool
was cut instantly in two.

'And now,' said Regin, seeing that Sigurd was
pleased, 'perhaps you will keep your promise and see
about Fafnir?'

'I gave no promise, Regin,' said the lad, 'and what
would the sons of Hunding say if they saw me getting
gold before avenging my father and my mother's father,
whom they slew?'

Before everything else, now that he had the sword,
Sigurd set forth with an army over the sea to finish
the destruction of Hunding which Helgi began. He
himself steered the dragon-ship, that was noblest in all
the fleet and had the most glorious coloured pictures
on its sails. A storm attacked them with foam on its
waves like blood, yet they refused even to shorten sail.
As they were passing close under a high sea-cliff, a tall
man standing on the edge in slouched hat and cloak,
very old but mighty, hailed them through the storm.
He asked who was their captain, and they answered,
' Sigurd, son of Sigmund, the most famous of the young
men.' ' You say truly,' said the tall man, ' there is none
like Sigurd among all the sons of kings. Will ye take me
on board ? ' First they asked his name, and he answered :
' They call me Nikar when I provide the ravens with
corpses ; but now you may call me Feng.'

Sigurd knew him, but still called him Nikar. When
he was on board, Sigurd asked him what were the truest
tokens of victory. The old man said that it was good
to be followed by a raven before battle, and to hear the
wolf howl under the ash-trees and to see it going before
you to battle ; and he added, ' No man should fight with
his face towards the sun when it is low ; let the enemy
look that way. Take care, too, that the warriors are
all sprucely combed, well washed, and well fed, in the
morning of battle ; for no one knows where his lodging
will be at night.' While Nikar was speaking the storm
sank asleep ; when they touched land in Hunding's
country he vanished.

Sigurd's army laid waste the country from the edge
of the sea onwards, until they were faced by Lyngi, the
king. Then a great battle was fought. Sword and axe
carved the flesh of men, spear and arrow pierced it.

Men that in the morning could speak, and think, and love, and run, and do a hundred different things, lay down before nightfall able to do nothing but feed the wolf, the raven, the rat, and the maggot. And all this was the work of sharp steel held in other men's hands. Good and bad, strong and weak, old and young, brave and cowardly, fell in heaps, and a few escaped. But because fewer of Sigurd's men fell than of Lyngi's, and Sigurd himself killed Lyngi, Sigurd had the victory. Those who were alive and unwounded on his side rejoiced; he got both honour and wealth, and was welcomed back with many feasts.

Regin did not forget Fafnir. He reminded Sigurd of the hoard, and Sigurd willingly rode up with him across Glistenheath to the dragon's drinking-place. Every evening the dragon used to go to a cliff above the river, and leaning out over it drank with ease of the water thirty fathoms below. Regin advised Sigurd to dig a hole at this place and wait in it until the dragon passed over the top; then he could stab it from below. Regin turned back before they had gone very far, leaving Sigurd to dig the pit, to wait, and to fight, alone.

While he was digging, a tall, bearded old man asked him what he was working at. When he knew, he advised Sigurd to dig several pits for the blood to run into, as well as one to sit in, lest he should be drowned in the blood. The old man vanished, and Sigurd dug several pits according to his advice. And it was well that he did. For when he had stabbed the dragon, the blood ran as if from a pump; nor could he move out for some time for fear of the coils that were lashing everywhere, more like three dragons than one. At last he slipped out and recovered his sword. The dying dragon asked Sigurd to tell him his name and his family. But dreading

lest Fafnir should curse him by his name, he pretended
to have none, until he was called a liar.   Then he
answered truthfully, 'Sigurd, the son of Sigmund.'
Fafnir did not curse him, but told him that he knew who
had persuaded him to seek the hoard : ' It was Regin,
my brother,' he said, ' that caused my death, and it is
my one joy that he will cause thy death also.   That
gold will be thy bane as it was mine.   Better would it be
for thee to ride away, for vengeance is sometimes taken
in spite of a death-wound.'

  ' I did not come here,' said Sigurd, ' to ask thy
counsel, but to win thy treasure.'

  ' Go, then, to my lair.   There is gold enough for all thy
life, and it shall be thy bane and the bane of every one
that owns it.'

  Sigurd answered :

  ' If I thought I should never die were I not to touch
that treasure, I would leave it behind me.   But I must die,
and, so long as he lives, a brave and true man can do well
with riches.'

  Fafnir said no more because he was dead.

  Regin welcomed back Sigurd from his victory, and
praised the deed.   Nevertheless, he wept a little for his
brother;   also he reminded Sigurd that the sword of
victory was of his making.   Sigurd laughed, because
Regin had been hiding with his face buried in the
heather during the fight.   When he cut out Fafnir's
heart Regin begged him to roast it and give him some
of it to eat.   Sigurd put the heart to roast before a fire.
Regin lay down and slept.   Presently, to try whether the
heart was well roasted, Sigurd dipped his finger in the
juice and tasted it.   The dragon's blood had magic in
it.   For, by that one taste, Sigurd gained the power to
understand the speech of all the birds.   Some magpies

were talking in the thorn-trees close by, and he heard one say :

' There sits the fool Sigurd covered with blood, and roasting the dragon's heart for somebody else.'

Another said :

' There lies Regin, thinking how he may get the treasure for himself.'

A third one said :

' Ye are both right. He had better give the ravens another meal.'

The fourth said :

' He will be a fool if he lets this other brother go free.'

So Sigurd cut off Regin's head and the birds knew that he had understood them, and they said to him out of the thorn-trees, as he sat looking at the fire and the roasting heart :

' Pick up thy gold, Sigurd. It is not kingly to listen to foreboding. There is a king's daughter waiting for thee, Brynhild, fairer than all others, and adorned with gold. She is in a golden hall that stands within a wall of flames on Hindfell. There she is sleeping. For Odin has put a spell upon her, because she, one of his Valkyries, destroyed one warrior and saved another against the will of the Gods.'

Sigurd took his eyes off the fire, and ate some of the heart and kept the rest. Then he mounted Grani and rode away to the cave of the treasure. It was cool now where the dragon had lain. Part of the gold was still in Otter's skin, for it had never been counted since Andwari lost it. Rodmar died before he had gone over all the rings and the coins and the jewels. Fafnir was too busy guarding them to count them, and he found, when he tried, that the high numbers soon sent him to sleep. Sigurd did not stop now to count the precious things. One ring he put upon his finger because of its brightness—the ring of the curse. He took also a corslet and a helmet of gold to wear. Two chests full of gold he put on Grani's back; until its master was mounted the horse seemed unable to move, but once it felt him in the saddle it galloped out of the cave and away.

II

Sigurd rode until he came in sight of Hindfell and a hedge of fire burning upon it. Inside the hedge of fire, as he came nearer, he saw a castle, and shields on the wall, and a banner on high. Grani galloped through the flames as if they had been waves, and Sigurd was untouched. At the castle gate he alighted, and entered with Gram, his sword. Not a sound could he hear as he went from room to room, except the hum of a bee that had lost its way. Nor did he see any other living thing until he came to a room where some one lay asleep in full armour. After waiting a little for the sleeper to awake, he noticed that a spider had spun a web between the helmet and the corslet, and that the spider lay dead in its web. Yet it was not a dead face that he found on taking off the helmet, but a living woman's. She slept as still and as close-wrapped in her corslet as a bud in winter. With his sword Sigurd slit open the corslet as if it had been cloth, and the woman emerged from it like a poppy-bud opening fast on a summer's day. She stretched herself, smiling with eyes that seemed to see nothing until she had closed them awhile and opened them again, and said:

'Who is this mighty one that has cut me free out of my sleep? Is it Sigurd, the son of Sigmund? Is that Fafnir's helmet on his head and Fafnir's bane, the sword Gram, in his hand?'

Sigurd answered :

' I am Sigurd, Sigmund's son, of the race of Volsung, and I have set thee free.'

She cried :

' I was enchanted by Odin. My sleep has been long, and never could I have broken out of it unhelped.'

' Art thou, then, Brynhild, the Valkyrie ? '

' I am Brynhild,' she said, but before speaking more to Sigurd she stood up to salute the day, and the night, and the Gods, and the earth, because now she could know them once more. Tall and fair she was, and bold as if she had been a sister of Thor. She was the daughter of a hero, fit to be the wife and the mother of heroes, and to be sung by poets. She told Sigurd how two kings were fighting, an old man named Helm Gunnar, and a younger named Agnar ; and Odin had promised Gunnar the victory, but she gave it to Agnar, so that he slew his enemy. Odin was angered at this. He surrounded her with shields, red and white, so that their rims touched and she could not escape. He pricked her with the thorn of sleep, and decreed that her sleep should only be broken by one who never felt fear. He planted the high flames round her castle, and decreed that only the man who brought with him Fafnir's gold should be able to ride through them. She was no longer to be a Valkyrie to fight, but a woman to be wedded like any other.

Sigurd asked her to teach him what she had learned as a Valkyrie.

' It may well be,' she said, ' that thou knowest already more than I. Yet what I know I will gladly teach. But first let us drink together, and mayst thou win glory by my teaching and never forget this day.'

When they had drunk together the cup of love, she said :

' Keep thy friends and thy kinsfolk, and overlook their faults and misdeeds.

' Take little notice of what fools say when there is a crowd and every one is talking ; for they say more than they mean.

' Nor take much notice either of what a drunken man says, and do not try to get the better of him by words.

' Trust not the friends or kinsfolk of those whom thou hast harmed.

' Go out into the open battle-field to fight thy foes ; do not wait to be burnt in thine own house.

' Do no wrong to the dead, and if thou find a dead man bid him sleep sweetly.

' Say what thou meanest, and keep thy word.

' Beware of evil. I cannot forecast long life for thee. Mighty feuds have arisen, and thou wilt be drawn into them.'

Sigurd loved her the more for her wisdom, and said : ' Brynhild, I will have thee for my own.' And she answered : ' I would choose thee out of all the sons of men.' And Sigurd and Brynhild swore to love one another.

Brynhild watched him ride away. He was tall and broad-shouldered in perfect proportion. His eyes were so keen that few dared look at them ; his hair was long and golden red; his beard short and thick, and of the same colour. He was the foremost of all heroes in the northern lands, good at battle, at speech, at sports, and at friendship ; the best of friends and the worst of enemies. He was young, and he thought he would live for ever and yet never be old. And he was right. For he never grew to be old, and he lives for ever in poets' books. While Brynhild watched him she almost forgot that he was her lover, because he was mightier-looking than a mortal man, like one of the heroes who lived for ever in the songs of the minstrels. She half believed that he was one of those heroes come back to earth; she half feared that he was only a vision. Certainly she had seen no one like him, as he rode away in his golden armour adorned with images of dragons, and a red dragon on his shield of gold.

He stopped first at the high house of a chief named Heimir, who had married Brynhild's sister, Bekkild, and had been foster-father to Brynhild herself. He stayed there riding and shooting with Heimir's son, Alswid. But one day when they were hawking Sigurd's hawk flew in at a window high in a tower, and he went up to fetch it. He passed many rooms before coming to the one he sought. In some he saw nothing; in one a sheet of blue sky through a window; in another armour; and in one a fair woman bending at needle-work, and so astonished was he that not until he had gone some way past did he know for certain that it was Brynhild he had seen. He turned back to look for the room, but somehow missed it, and came down again to Alswid without his hawk.

'What is the matter?' asked Alswid, and Sigurd told him.

'Yes,' said Alswid, 'that was Brynhild, Budli's daughter, the noblest of noble women. She came here not long after thee. Do not let her trouble thy heart. She will love no man.'

Nevertheless, next day Sigurd found her room, and came to her where she sat working a picture of gold on a cloth, and the picture was of Sigurd and the dragon and the dragon's hoard. He asked her if all was well with her, and she said it was, but said also that no one can tell how long good fortune will last. Sigurd sat down

at her side. Presently four maidens entered, carrying
large goblets of wine. Brynhild stood up and offered one
to him, bidding him welcome and to drink the wine.
First he took the goblet and set it down, and then took
her hand and drew her towards him, and put his arms
about her neck and kissed her, saying :

'Thou art fairest ! '

'Ah,' said Brynhild, ' is it wise to trust in women ?
For they often break their words.'

'The day that made us both happy together would
be the best of days,' said Sigurd.

'But I,' said she, ' am a war maid, and it is not fated
that we shall dwell together.'

'Then there is nothing in life,' said he.

'Yes, but there is,' said she, ' for me the battle ; for
thee, Gudrun, the daughter of Giuki, for a wife.'

'No, no ! ' he cried, ' I can never forget thee. No
king's daughter shall steal away my thoughts from thee.
I swear now that either I will have thee for my own, or
I will have no one.'

Brynhild would say no more. She looked kindly and
sorrowfully at Sigurd. She took the gold ring that he
gave her so fondly that she seemed to forget what she had
been saying. Sigurd did forget everything, except her
kind looks and his ring on her finger. No man now was
more joyous than he in the chase and at the feast.

Brynhild sat on in her tower sewing at the picture of
Sigurd and Fafnir, and Fafnir's hoard. Few came to see
her, and she desired no one that came. But one day
a large company of women was seen coming towards the
castle in gilded chariots. ' That will be Gudrun, Giuki's
daughter, fairest of women,' said Brynhild on hearing
the news; ' let us go out to meet her.' So they went
out and greeted Gudrun and her company, and led her

into the hall and waited upon her. But Gudrun said hardly anything. Brynhild chided her gently, saying :

'Let us talk about the greatest kings and heroes, and the deeds they have done.'

'What kings,' asked Gudrun suddenly, 'dost thou think the greatest?'

And Brynhild answered :

'The sons of Haki.'

'They are great men in their way, yet Sigar took away one of their sisters and burnt the other with her house, nor have they taken revenge. I think my own brothers are greater than these.'

'They are men of the greatest promise, but they have so far done little ; and there is one who is far before them —Sigurd, the son of Sigmund, who slew his father's slayers, and put an end to Fafnir and took away his hoard.'

'How dost thou know these things ? But I know how it is ; it is through love. Now I will tell thee why I came here ; it was to tell thee a dream that has grieved me.'

'Be not troubled by dreams, but stay with thy friends and let them see thee happy as they would wish.'

'Thou art like my woman, who said when I told her that I had had a dream that grieved me, "I shall gladly hear it, because you can often tell the weather from a dream." This is no weather dream. I dreamed that I had a golden hawk on my wrist, and that I gave up everything for the sake of the hawk. The woman said this meant that some goodly king's son was waiting for my love. But she could tell me no more, so I said, "Let us go to Brynhild. She is wise, and perhaps she will tell us more." The next night I dreamed that I and many others went out from the bower, and saw a hart fairer than all others and golden-haired. All of us

desired him, but I had him. Yet I had him for a
moment only. Even as he stood at my knees an arrow
pierced him and slew him. Thine, Brynhild, thine was
the arrow; and in the dream thou gavest me instead
of the hart a wolf-cub that sprinkled me with my
brothers' blood.'

Brynhild looked kindly enough at Gudrun as she told
her the meaning of the dream :

' Sigurd,' she said, ' shall come to thee, and thou shalt
have him, though I have chosen him for my own. For
thy mother, Grimhild, shall put something in his drink.
Quickly shalt thou wed him, and quickly lose him.
Afterwards thou shalt wed my brother, King Atli, who
shall slay thy brothers. But in the end thou shalt slay
Atli.'

' Would that I had never known such things,' wept
Gudrun, and turned away.

' Weep, Gudrun,' said Brynhild, ' and weeping will
wash away thy knowledge. If thou art afraid of the
truth, thou wilt soon forget it with a little weeping and
a little laughter.'

But Gudrun did not hear these words. The sight of
Sigurd riding into her father's courtyard not long after
this would have made her forget greater woes than ever
came from a dream. One of the men in the courtyard
ran in to King Giuki, shouting :

' There is one of the Gods in our courtyard, though
which of them it is I cannot think. For Balder is dead,
and this one is better-looking and younger than Odin
or Thor. He is all over gold. His horse is a horse indeed.
His weapons are wonderful : the sword pricks your
finger if you look at it.'

Giuki went out, pretending to be used to such
wonders, for he was a great king, and at first he said :

' Who art thou riding in here so free ? Have my sons given thee leave ? '

' I am called Sigurd,' answered the God-like man.

' Then welcome,' said Giuki at once; ' everything here is at thy service.'

Gudrun was watching from a window, but when Sigurd looked up he saw only a pigeon courting on the roof-top. He made friends at once with Giuki's sons, Gunnar and Hogni. He rode out with them here and there, and in all feats of strength and skill he excelled them. Their mother, Grimhild, soon learned from them that he loved Brynhild, for he often talked of her. Grimhild liked him, and thought that she would like him better still as a son-in-law, because he was so powerful and had such wealth. So she plotted to bring about a marriage between Sigurd and Gudrun. One night at a feast she offered him a horn to drink from with her own hands. He took it as he would have taken any other horn, and as he drank, Grimhild looked steadily at him, saying in a quiet voice several times :

' Thy father shall be Giuki and I shall be thy mother. Thy brothers shall be Gunnar and Hogni.'

When Sigurd heard her saying these words for the last time, as he finished drinking, he said :

' So shall it be. There could be nothing better.' For that drink had taken away from him all memory of Brynhild.

Giuki knew nothing of this, nor did Grimhild tell him. But one day she spoke to him very lovingly for some time, and then gradually turned the talk to Sigurd, saying that Giuki ought to give his daughter to Sigurd and so keep him with them for ever. Giuki had not heard before of kings offering their daughters in this way, but Grimhild persuaded and persuaded him, until he thought there could be no harm in offering Gudrun to one like Sigurd. Hogni and Gunnar knew of the plan, and they sometimes talked of Gudrun to Sigurd. But Sigurd liked her well enough after the drink and Grimhild's words in the hall. The maid herself had poured out his wine for him on the night after, and he loved her as she bent over the cup, watching the wine for fear of spilling it, yet filling it too full for all her watching. Therefore it easily came about that Sigurd married Gudrun. He and her two brothers swore brotherhood, and they lived together and fought together, and the glory of each one was the glory of all. Gudrun pleased Sigurd well; and he gave her some of Fafnir's heart to eat, which made her bold and wise as well as loving-kind; and they had a son whom they called Sigmund.

III

Grimhild was satisfied for a time. Then she thought of one thing more to make the family power and happiness complete. If only Gunnar could marry Brynhild! Soon every one was speaking of this. Even Sigurd joined in urging Gunnar to woo Brynhild. Moreover, when Gunnar set out for the house of King Budli, Brynhild's father, Sigurd was in his company. Budli was willing for Gunnar to have Brynhild, if Brynhild was willing to have him; for, said he, 'She is proud and has her own way.' Heimir, her foster-father, said the same thing, and that she would not have any one who had not ridden to her through the hedge of flames. They now rode to Brynhild's castle. The hedge still grew high all round it, too high to be leaped and too thick to be pierced by ordinary riders. Gunnar's horse would not look at the flames, though he struck it fiercely.

Sigurd lent him his own horse Grani, but Grani stood still with Gunnar in the saddle. Then Sigurd took on the likeness of Gunnar and gave Gunnar his own, and mounted the horse. Grani knew who was riding him, and ran straight ahead, though the earth shook and the flames towered up above the castle as if they would break loose from the earth and touch the sky. Grani remembered his first ride, but Sigurd forgot. Now for the second time Sigurd went into the castle up to Brynhild's chamber, where she sat with her corslet and helmet on, and her sword in her hand. She looked at him without love, asking him who he was, and he answered that he was Gunnar, and that he had earned her for his wife by riding through the flames. She knew not how to answer him, except by murmuring that she thought Sigurd alone could have done that, and Sigurd was her betrothed already. She consented to marry him only to keep her word, and sadly she consented. When he had given her a ring and she had given him back the ring of the curse, he left her, and, returning to his proper shape, he told Gunnar what had happened. Brynhild was to come soon to King Giuki's court. On her way she told her foster-father the news :

' The man rode through the fire and said that he came a-wooing, and his name was Gunnar ; and I said that only Sigurd could have done this, and that I had been betrothed to Sigurd before and loved him.'

Her foster-father said :

' What must be must be.'

Next she went to her father Budli's castle, and Budli accompanied her to Giuki's court with Atli, his son. They had a great welcome, and Brynhild married Gunnar. And now in some way it came to pass that Sigurd remembered Brynhild, how he had loved her and

sworn to be hers. He said no word of this to any man,
but only to Gudrun.

One day Brynhild and Gudrun were bathing together
in the broad river, and Brynhild swam far out beyond
Gudrun. So when she came back Gudrun asked her :

'Why didst thou swim out beyond me ? Was it a
boast ? '

'I meant nothing by it,' said Brynhild, 'though maybe
I am the better swimmer to-day.'

'Thou mayst well boast of swimming, for thou hast
nothing else to boast of.'

'I do not boast, yet the fact is I have much to boast
of, if I wished. My father is a more mighty king than
thine. My husband also—*thy* brother—has done greater
deeds than thine. He rode through the flaming hedge,
but thy Sigurd was once thrall to King Hialprek.'

'Thou art alone in speaking thus of Sigurd. Thou
knowest better than any one that it is not true. He
slew Fafnir. He rode through the flames to thee once,
as well thou knowest. What is more, he rode through
the flames a second time, which thou didst not know,
and here is the proof of it.'

So saying, Gudrun showed her the ring of the curse.
Brynhild went white as death at sight of the ring, nor
could she speak for the thoughts that came into her
mind.

Day after day Brynhild went sadly about, and
Gudrun pitied her. She asked Sigurd if she should go
to Brynhild, but though he said 'No' she went. She told
Brynhild that she was sorry for what she had said in
the river. Yet as soon as Brynhild spoke her mind
Gudrun lost her temper, taunting her, and telling her that
she had been cast off by Sigurd.

Brynhild was no better for these words. Her sadness

made her ill, and she took to her bed. For a long time she would not answer Gunnar when he asked her what was the matter. But being questioned over and over again, she said at last :

'Where is the ring I gave thee ? . . . No, do not trouble to answer, lest thou mightest lie as already thou hast done. Alas! I also have lied. For I promised to wed the man who could ride through the flames to me, which only Sigurd could do. Yet he is not my husband, though he rode twice through the flames, but thou art, who dared not come through them once. I have broken my vow that I would marry only the noblest man alive. But I will be the death of thee, Gunnar, and I will reward well thy mother Grimhild.'

She would have slain him, if Hogni, his brother, had not seized her and fettered her. But Gunnar would not have her kept in fetters, hoping that if she were free she would recover and live her life with him as before. She read his thoughts, for she cried :

'It will not profit thee to loose me. Thou wilt never again see me glad in the hall, or drinking wine, or playing at chess, or joining in cheerful talk, or embroidering, or sharing thy counsels. Thou didst take away Sigurd from me and put thyself in his place.'

She destroyed her needlework, and she cried aloud so that every one could hear her and many could not help weeping with her. Then her room became silent; no one saw her or heard her for several days. Gudrun inquired after her, and she was told that Brynhild was lying quite still and silent, and was neither eating nor drinking. She bade Gunnar go to his wife, but he would not, for he knew that he was not wanted. Hogni consented to go, and got not a word from Brynhild. Then all prayed Sigurd to go to her. At first he said nothing,

for he knew Brynhild was in a brooding fury against him.
But in the end he went at the request of Gudrun. Seeing
Brynhild, as he supposed, asleep, he cried :

'Awake, Brynhild ! come out into the sun and cast
off this dreaminess and grief.'

She turned quickly round and looked at him, with these
words :

'And does even Sigurd dare to come and look at me ? '

'Why,' he asked, 'why wilt thou not speak to any
one ? what is the use ? '

'I will not hide my anger from thee,' she said.

'Thou art under a spell,' he answered, 'if thou
thinkest that I have any evil intention against thee.
Besides, thou hast the husband thou didst choose.'

'Do not say such things. Thou knowest that Gunnar
never rode through the flames to me. Even at the time
I wondered, for I saw that the man had thine eyes.'

'Yet there are no better men than Giuki's sons.'

'They did not slay Fafnir, nor ride through the fire for
my sake.'

'But I am not thy husband.'

'Nor has Gunnar my love.'

'Yet he deserves it. But tell me what is the cause
of thy anger now, for these things are past and cannot
be changed.'

For a moment Brynhild paused. Then she said
fiercely :

'What angers me most now is that I have not yet seen
the sword red with thy blood, Sigurd.'

'Oh, Brynhild, then I shall soon take away thy anger,
if my heart's blood can do it. Yet I think thou wilt
not profit much by that, for thou wilt not live long
after I am dead.'

'I care not for thy life or thy death.'

' Then live, and love King Gunnar and me also, and
I will do all that I can. To change the past I am
powerless. I also have sorrowed for it, but until now
I was thinking that sorrow had ceased, and I was beginning to be glad that at least Brynhild was not far off.
Yet even now, if it please thee, I will put away Gudrun
and wed thee, rather than let thee die.'

As he spoke these words his breast so heaved with
sorrow that the rings of his corslet were snapped. But
Brynhild said :

' I will not have thee, nor any man.'

Thus Sigurd left her, for no more could he say.

Outside he met Gunnar, who asked him whether
Brynhild could speak. ' Yes, she can speak,' he answered.

When Gunnar came to her room she was crying out :
' I am loveless, husbandless, soulless.' To Gunnar she
said :

' Gunnar, thou wilt lose me and all that I have. I will
go back home again, and I will sit and dream my life out
alone if thou wilt not do what I ask.'

' What is that ? '

' Kill Sigurd. He has been talking to Gudrun. Listen.
Sigurd, or Gunnar, or Brynhild must die. Thou shalt
choose.'

For a long time Gunnar went about thinking sadly.
He did not want to lose Brynhild and her dowry, or
to kill Sigurd. He would have liked to have Sigurd's
treasure ; on the other hand, he had sworn brotherhood
with Sigurd. At the end of the day he was thinking
exactly as he had done at the beginning, so he consulted
Hogni, his brother. Hogni was no more willing than
Gunnar to break his oath with Sigurd. He blamed
Brynhild. For he guessed that she had egged on her
husband, in her jealousy of Gudrun. Presently Gunnar

said that their young brother, Guttorm, might do the
deed, since he had never sworn brotherhood with Sigurd.
So they offered Guttorm great rewards and honours, and
to make all sure they gave him a dish of the flesh of a
wolf and a snake. Sure enough, Guttorm grew very eager
to use his sword. He went in to Sigurd in the very early
morning, but finding him with his eyes open, staring at
something, he slipped out in alarm. A second time he
failed in the same way. But the third time the bright
eyes were closed, and Guttorm thrust his sword clean
through into the bed below. He had his reward immediately. Sigurd rose up in the pangs of death and
threw his sword Gram at the murderer, cutting him in
two. The hero's blood awoke Gudrun, and sharper than
the sword were her sighs. He tried to comfort her :

'Our son is alive,' he said, 'and as to my enemies,
they have done themselves little good. It was Brynhild's
plot. She persuaded Gunnar, yet I never harmed him.'

He could speak no more, and in a little while Gudrun
knew that he was dead. One shriek, that made the cups
rattle on the wall and the geese scream in the yard,
was all the sound she made. She did not cry or wring
her hands, but she sat still and near to death. Wise
men came to lighten her heavy heart, but could not.
The women tried to comfort her by recalling their
own sorrows : how they had lost husbands—one of them
had lost five husbands—sisters, brothers, and children ;
how they had been insulted and taken captive and left
alone. Still Gudrun could not weep beside the bed. It
was Goldbrand, Gunnar's sister, who thought of a way.
She uncovered Sigurd's body, letting the sheet fall on
the ground close to Gudrun's feet, which made Gudrun
lift her eyes. At the sight of the breast and the sword-
hole, the hair dripping with blood, the keen eyes dead,

she fell upon the pillow with cheeks reddened and tears trickling like mist drops in a wood.

'The love of ye two,' said Goldbrand, ' is the greatest I ever saw upon earth. Thou couldst never rest, my sister, indoors or out, except at Sigurd's side.'

The women praised Sigurd, for his strength, for his courage, for his beauty, for his great deeds, and for his generosity ; and Gudrun raised her head to say :

'There was no one like him. None. It was my brothers' fault that he died, but they shall not gain by it. O that Sigurd had never ridden with them to Brynhild's castle ! '

Brynhild knew the moment of Sigurd's death by Gudrun's loud shriek. When she heard that shriek she laughed once, but only once.

Gunnar did not like the whiteness of her face. ' Not for joy thou laughest, Brynhild,' said he, ' nor for anything good.'

' Oh, well done, Gunnar. Thou hast slain Sigurd in his bed, or at least one has done it for thee. I wish thee joy of thy deed, since thou hast slain the keen king. It is well for thee he is dead, who would have ruled everything as he chose if he had lived much longer. He was the only man that ever I loved. When I saw him sitting with his treasure on Grani's back I loved him. Gunnar, thine eyes are like an old man's. They are not like Sigurd's, nor is there any part of thee equal to Sigurd. He was Gudrun's husband, but now he is not, and no one can forbid me to love him. He spoke truly, I think, when he said that I should not live long after his death.'

With these words and much weeping, Brynhild sank down. Fearing that she would take her own life, Gunnar put his arms round her neck ; but suddenly she grew strong and cast him off, nor would she let any one else come near her. Gunnar called Hogni to advise him how to save Brynhild from herself. ' Let no man save her,' said Hogni, ' she has done nothing but evil, and never will.' She was silent now, dealing out her treasures to the bondmaids and women of the house. She kept back a golden mail-coat and put it on, and then, when no one was expecting it, she thrust herself through with a sword. What treasures were still left she dealt out among the women as she lay bleeding. Then she began to speak to the men in the hall, and chiefly to Gunnar :

' Will ye listen to me now that I am almost dead ? For it is a strange custom among men to listen to men when they have perchance lost half their wit in the pangs of death, rather than when they are alive and strong in every way. I can tell ye things that I think ye do not know. Gunnar will be friendly again with Gudrun ere long. Gudrun shall bear a child called Swanhild, as beautiful as the light of the sun. Gudrun shall marry a second husband, my brother Atli, but against her will. Thou, Gunnar, wilt desire to wed my sister Ordrun, but Atli will not permit it, and will cast thee into a pit of snakes. Gudrun shall slay· Atli. She shall oftentimes wish before the end that she had done as I have done now. A third time she shall marry, to King Jonakr, and bear him sons. As for Swanhild, the last of Sigurd's race, she shall be trodden under by horses.

' Now grant me this one boon. Make a broad funeral pyre on the plain, big enough for all of us who are going to die with Sigurd. Deck it with shields and red cloths from Gaul. Burn me on one side of Sigurd, and five bondmaids, decked with necklaces, on the other. Put two menservants at our feet and two at our head, with my nurse, my fosterer, and two horses, two hounds, and two hawks. Lay a sharp sword between us two. We shall be a goodly company yonder. I can say no more.'

Thus Brynhild died and was burnt on the pyre with Sigurd.

Gudrun went out into the forest alone. The wolves howled, and she wished that they would make an end of her. But she wandered unharmed until she came after many days to a hospitable hall. Long she lived with Thora, the King of Denmark's daughter, embroidering pictures of battles, and especially the deeds of Sigurd, and his warriors with swords and helmets, and his ships with gilt figure-heads and carved bows. At last this life came to an end. Three kings courted her, but she refused them and their gifts. Then her mother Grimhild, with a cold and bitter drink, persuaded her to appease Atli, Brynhild's brother, by marrying him, though she hated him and foresaw that he would one day be the death of her brothers. Gudrun warned them, but so it turned out, as Brynhild also had prophesied. Gunnar came wooing Atli's sister Ordrun against his will, and Atli made this an excuse to slay both Gunnar and Hogni. With them the treasure of Fafnir was lost, which Atli had hoped to gain. The brothers had buried it in the Rhine, and no one but they knew the place, nor ever did know thereafter. Gudrun did not leave them unavenged. She slew her own children, Atli's children. She gave Atli wine to drink that was mingled with their blood, and when he was drunk with it she slew him and burnt down his hall with every one and everything in it. She had only Swanhild left, and to save her she married King Jonakr the Hun. For some time they lived in peace. Swanhild married Ermanarik, King of the Goths; Gudrun bore sons to Jonakr. Then news came that Ermanarik had

caused Swanhild to be trodden to death by horses
because of a story against her. Gudrun urged the three
sons of Jonakr to revenge their sister. She herself chose
their helmets and mail-coats. They shook out their
cloaks, fastened on their swords, and leapt angrily
on to their horses. They rode over the wet mountains
foaming with rage, to certain death. On the way they
quarrelled, and one was killed, but the other two
rode on.

Ermanarik was in his hall, smiling with wine and
stroking his brown beard, and smiling all the more because he had heard that the brothers were coming. They
burst in and began to slay, and Ermanarik only smiled,
because the wine made him unable to do anything else.
He laughed aloud, crying : ' Cannot a thousand Goths
kill or bind two lone men in our hall ? ' But no sword
would cut the sons of Jonakr on that day, and they slew
all that opposed them, and they cut off the king's hands
and feet. Then came into the hall an old man, very tall
and one-eyed, telling the Goths not to use cutting weapons,
but stones. So they threw stones until the brothers were
killed. Thus Gudrun was left alone. It was not long
before a funeral pile was made for her. In her last hours
she called out for Sigurd to come on his white horse,
bidding him remember what they had promised one
another when they were first wedded, that Sigurd should
come to her out of Hell even, if she called him, and that
she should go down to Hell to him if he called her. ' Pile
up the oak-branches,' she cried ; ' let the pile stand
high. May my sorrow-laden breast burn, may the
flames make all clean again, and in them may my
sorrow melt away.'

A CATALOG OF SELECTED
DOVER BOOKS
IN ALL FIELDS OF INTEREST

A CATALOG OF SELECTED DOVER
BOOKS IN ALL FIELDS OF INTEREST

CONCERNING THE SPIRITUAL IN ART, Wassily Kandinsky. Pioneering work by father of abstract art. Thoughts on color theory, nature of art. Analysis of earlier masters. 12 illustrations. 80pp. of text. 5⅜ x 8½. 0-486-23411-8

CELTIC ART: The Methods of Construction, George Bain. Simple geometric techniques for making Celtic interlacements, spirals, Kells-type initials, animals, humans, etc. Over 500 illustrations. 160pp. 9 x 12. (Available in U.S. only.) 0-486-22923-8

AN ATLAS OF ANATOMY FOR ARTISTS, Fritz Schider. Most thorough reference work on art anatomy in the world. Hundreds of illustrations, including selections from works by Vesalius, Leonardo, Goya, Ingres, Michelangelo, others. 593 illustrations. 192pp. 7⅛ x 10¼. 0-486-20241-0

CELTIC HAND STROKE-BY-STROKE (Irish Half-Uncial from "The Book of Kells"): An Arthur Baker Calligraphy Manual, Arthur Baker. Complete guide to creating each letter of the alphabet in distinctive Celtic manner. Covers hand position, strokes, pens, inks, paper, more. Illustrated. 48pp. 8¼ x 11. 0-486-24336-2

EASY ORIGAMI, John Montroll. Charming collection of 32 projects (hat, cup, pelican, piano, swan, many more) specially designed for the novice origami hobbyist. Clearly illustrated easy-to-follow instructions insure that even beginning papercrafters will achieve successful results. 48pp. 8¼ x 11. 0-486-27298-2

BLOOMINGDALE'S ILLUSTRATED 1886 CATALOG: Fashions, Dry Goods and Housewares, Bloomingdale Brothers. Famed merchants' extremely rare catalog depicting about 1,700 products: clothing, housewares, firearms, dry goods, jewelry, more. Invaluable for dating, identifying vintage items. Also, copyright-free graphics for artists, designers. Co-published with Henry Ford Museum & Greenfield Village. 160pp. 8¼ x 11. 0-486-25780-0

THE ART OF WORLDLY WISDOM, Baltasar Gracian. "Think with the few and speak with the many," "Friends are a second existence," and "Be able to forget" are among this 1637 volume's 300 pithy maxims. A perfect source of mental and spiritual refreshment, it can be opened at random and appreciated either in brief or at length. 128pp. 5⅜ x 8½. 0-486-44034-6

JOHNSON'S DICTIONARY: A Modern Selection, Samuel Johnson (E. L. McAdam and George Milne, eds.). This modern version reduces the original 1755 edition's 2,300 pages of definitions and literary examples to a more manageable length, retaining the verbal pleasure and historical curiosity of the original. 480pp. 5⁵⁄₁₆ x 8¼. 0-486-44089-3

ADVENTURES OF HUCKLEBERRY FINN, Mark Twain, Illustrated by E. W. Kemble. A work of eternal richness and complexity, a source of ongoing critical debate, and a literary landmark, Twain's 1885 masterpiece about a barefoot boy's journey of self-discovery has enthralled readers around the world. This handsome clothbound reproduction of the first edition features all 174 of the original black-and-white illustrations. 368pp. 5⅜ x 8½. 0-486-44322-1

STICKLEY CRAFTSMAN FURNITURE CATALOGS, Gustav Stickley and L. & J. G. Stickley. Beautiful, functional furniture in two authentic catalogs from 1910. 594 illustrations, including 277 photos, show settles, rockers, armchairs, reclining chairs, bookcases, desks, tables. 183pp. 6½ x 9¼. 0-486-23838-5

AMERICAN LOCOMOTIVES IN HISTORIC PHOTOGRAPHS: 1858 to 1949, Ron Ziel (ed.). A rare collection of 126 meticulously detailed official photographs, called "builder portraits," of American locomotives that majestically chronicle the rise of steam locomotive power in America. Introduction. Detailed captions. xi+ 129pp. 9 x 12. 0-486-27393-8

AMERICA'S LIGHTHOUSES: An Illustrated History, Francis Ross Holland, Jr. Delightfully written, profusely illustrated fact-filled survey of over 200 American light-houses since 1716. History, anecdotes, technological advances, more. 240pp. 8 x 10¾. 0-486-25576-X

TOWARDS A NEW ARCHITECTURE, Le Corbusier. Pioneering manifesto by founder of "International School." Technical and aesthetic theories, views of industry, eco-nomics, relation of form to function, "mass-production split" and much more. Profusely illustrated. 320pp. 6⅛ x 9¼. (Available in U.S. only.) 0-486-25023-7

HOW THE OTHER HALF LIVES, Jacob Riis. Famous journalistic record, expos-ing poverty and degradation of New York slums around 1900, by major social reformer. 100 striking and influential photographs. 233pp. 10 x 7⅞. 0-486-22012-5

FRUIT KEY AND TWIG KEY TO TREES AND SHRUBS, William M. Harlow. One of the handiest and most widely used identification aids. Fruit key covers 120 deciduous and evergreen species; twig key 160 deciduous species. Easily used. Over 300 photographs. 126pp. 5⅜ x 8½. 0-486-20511-8

COMMON BIRD SONGS, Dr. Donald J. Borror. Songs of 60 most common U.S. birds: robins, sparrows, cardinals, bluejays, finches, more—arranged in order of increasing complexity. Up to 9 variations of songs of each species.
Cassette and manual 0-486-99911-4

ORCHIDS AS HOUSE PLANTS, Rebecca Tyson Northen. Grow cattleyas and many other kinds of orchids—in a window, in a case, or under artificial light. 63 illus-trations. 148pp. 5⅜ x 8½. 0-486-23261-1

MONSTER MAZES, Dave Phillips. Masterful mazes at four levels of difficulty. Avoid deadly perils and evil creatures to find magical treasures. Solutions for all 32 exciting illustrated puzzles. 48pp. 8¼ x 11. 0-486-26005-4

MOZART'S DON GIOVANNI (DOVER OPERA LIBRETTO SERIES), Wolfgang Amadeus Mozart. Introduced and translated by Ellen H. Bleiler. Standard Italian libretto, with complete English translation. Convenient and thoroughly portable—an ideal companion for reading along with a recording or the performance itself. Introduction. List of characters. Plot summary. 121pp. 5¼ x 8½. 0-486-24944-1

FRANK LLOYD WRIGHT'S DANA HOUSE, Donald Hoffmann. Pictorial essay of residential masterpiece with over 160 interior and exterior photos, plans, eleva-tions, sketches and studies. 128pp. 9¼ x 10¾. 0-486-29120-0

THE CLARINET AND CLARINET PLAYING, David Pino. Lively, comprehensive work features suggestions about technique, musicianship, and musical interpretation, as well as guidelines for teaching, making your own reeds, and preparing for public performance. Includes an intriguing look at clarinet history. "A godsend," *The Clarinet,* Journal of the International Clarinet Society. Appendixes. 7 illus. 320pp. 5⅜ x 8½. 0-486-40270-3

HOLLYWOOD GLAMOR PORTRAITS, John Kobal (ed.). 145 photos from 1926-49. Harlow, Gable, Bogart, Bacall; 94 stars in all. Full background on photographers, technical aspects. 160pp. 8⅜ x 11¼. 0-486-23352-9

THE RAVEN AND OTHER FAVORITE POEMS, Edgar Allan Poe. Over 40 of the author's most memorable poems: "The Bells," "Ulalume," "Israfel," "To Helen," "The Conqueror Worm," "Eldorado," "Annabel Lee," many more. Alphabetic lists of titles and first lines. 64pp. 5$^{3}/_{16}$ x 8¼. 0-486-26685-0

PERSONAL MEMOIRS OF U. S. GRANT, Ulysses Simpson Grant. Intelligent, deeply moving firsthand account of Civil War campaigns, considered by many the finest military memoirs ever written. Includes letters, historic photographs, maps and more. 528pp. 6⅛ x 9¼. 0-486-28587-1

ANCIENT EGYPTIAN MATERIALS AND INDUSTRIES, A. Lucas and J. Harris. Fascinating, comprehensive, thoroughly documented text describes this ancient civilization's vast resources and the processes that incorporated them in daily life, including the use of animal products, building materials, cosmetics, perfumes and incense, fibers, glazed ware, glass and its manufacture, materials used in the mummification process, and much more. 544pp. 6⅛ x 9¼. (Available in U.S. only.) 0-486-40446-3

RUSSIAN STORIES/RUSSKIE RASSKAZY: A Dual-Language Book, edited by Gleb Struve. Twelve tales by such masters as Chekhov, Tolstoy, Dostoevsky, Pushkin, others. Excellent word-for-word English translations on facing pages, plus teaching and study aids, Russian/English vocabulary, biographical/critical introductions, more. 416pp. 5⅜ x 8½. 0-486-26244-8

PHILADELPHIA THEN AND NOW: 60 Sites Photographed in the Past and Present, Kenneth Finkel and Susan Oyama. Rare photographs of City Hall, Logan Square, Independence Hall, Betsy Ross House, other landmarks juxtaposed with contemporary views. Captures changing face of historic city. Introduction. Captions. 128pp. 8¼ x 11. 0-486-25790-8

NORTH AMERICAN INDIAN LIFE: Customs and Traditions of 23 Tribes, Elsie Clews Parsons (ed.). 27 fictionalized essays by noted anthropologists examine religion, customs, government, additional facets of life among the Winnebago, Crow, Zuni, Eskimo, other tribes. 480pp. 6⅛ x 9¼. 0-486-27377-6

TECHNICAL MANUAL AND DICTIONARY OF CLASSICAL BALLET, Gail Grant. Defines, explains, comments on steps, movements, poses and concepts. 15-page pictorial section. Basic book for student, viewer. 127pp. 5⅜ x 8½. 0-486-21843-0

THE MALE AND FEMALE FIGURE IN MOTION: 60 Classic Photographic Sequences, Eadweard Muybridge. 60 true-action photographs of men and women walking, running, climbing, bending, turning, etc., reproduced from rare 19th-century masterpiece. vi + 121pp. 9 x 12. 0-486-24745-7

ANIMALS: 1,419 Copyright-Free Illustrations of Mammals, Birds, Fish, Insects, etc., Jim Harter (ed.). Clear wood engravings present, in extremely lifelike poses, over 1,000 species of animals. One of the most extensive pictorial sourcebooks of its kind. Captions. Index. 284pp. 9 x 12. 0-486-23766-4

1001 QUESTIONS ANSWERED ABOUT THE SEASHORE, N. J. Berrill and Jacquelyn Berrill. Queries answered about dolphins, sea snails, sponges, starfish, fishes, shore birds, many others. Covers appearance, breeding, growth, feeding, much more. 305pp. 5¼ x 8¼. 0-486-23366-9

ATTRACTING BIRDS TO YOUR YARD, William J. Weber. Easy-to-follow guide offers advice on how to attract the greatest diversity of birds: birdhouses, feeders, water and waterers, much more. 96pp. 5³⁄₁₆ x 8¼. 0-486-28927-3

MEDICINAL AND OTHER USES OF NORTH AMERICAN PLANTS: A Historical Survey with Special Reference to the Eastern Indian Tribes, Charlotte Erichsen-Brown. Chronological historical citations document 500 years of usage of plants, trees, shrubs native to eastern Canada, northeastern U.S. Also complete identifying information. 343 illustrations. 544pp. 6½ x 9¼. 0-486-25951-X

STORYBOOK MAZES, Dave Phillips. 23 stories and mazes on two-page spreads: Wizard of Oz, Treasure Island, Robin Hood, etc. Solutions. 64pp. 8¼ x 11. 0-486-23628-5

AMERICAN NEGRO SONGS: 230 Folk Songs and Spirituals, Religious and Secular, John W. Work. This authoritative study traces the African influences of songs sung and played by black Americans at work, in church, and as entertainment. The author discusses the lyric significance of such songs as "Swing Low, Sweet Chariot," "John Henry," and others and offers the words and music for 230 songs. Bibliography. Index of Song Titles. 272pp. 6½ x 9¼. 0-486-40271-1

MOVIE-STAR PORTRAITS OF THE FORTIES, John Kobal (ed.). 163 glamor, studio photos of 106 stars of the 1940s: Rita Hayworth, Ava Gardner, Marlon Brando, Clark Gable, many more. 176pp. 8⅜ x 11¼. 0-486-23546-7

YEKL and THE IMPORTED BRIDEGROOM AND OTHER STORIES OF YIDDISH NEW YORK, Abraham Cahan. Film Hester Street based on *Yekl* (1896). Novel, other stories among first about Jewish immigrants on N.Y.'s East Side. 240pp. 5⅜ x 8½. 0-486-22427-9

SELECTED POEMS, Walt Whitman. Generous sampling from *Leaves of Grass*. Twenty-four poems include "I Hear America Singing," "Song of the Open Road," "I Sing the Body Electric," "When Lilacs Last in the Dooryard Bloom'd," "O Captain! My Captain!"—all reprinted from an authoritative edition. Lists of titles and first lines. 128pp. 5³⁄₁₆ x 8¼. 0-486-26878-0

SONGS OF EXPERIENCE: Facsimile Reproduction with 26 Plates in Full Color, William Blake. 26 full-color plates from a rare 1826 edition. Includes "The Tyger," "London," "Holy Thursday," and other poems. Printed text of poems. 48pp. 5¼ x 7. 0-486-24636-1

THE BEST TALES OF HOFFMANN, E. T. A. Hoffmann. 10 of Hoffmann's most important stories: "Nutcracker and the King of Mice," "The Golden Flowerpot," etc. 458pp. 5⅜ x 8½. 0-486-21793-0

THE BOOK OF TEA, Kakuzo Okakura. Minor classic of the Orient: entertaining, charming explanation, interpretation of traditional Japanese culture in terms of tea ceremony. 94pp. 5⅜ x 8½. 0-486-20070-1

FRENCH STORIES/CONTES FRANÇAIS: A Dual-Language Book, Wallace Fowlie. Ten stories by French masters, Voltaire to Camus: "Micromegas" by Voltaire; "The Atheist's Mass" by Balzac; "Minuet" by de Maupassant; "The Guest" by Camus, six more. Excellent English translations on facing pages. Also French-English vocabulary list, exercises, more. 352pp. 5⅜ x 8½. 0-486-26443-2

CHICAGO AT THE TURN OF THE CENTURY IN PHOTOGRAPHS: 122 Historic Views from the Collections of the Chicago Historical Society, Larry A. Viskochil. Rare large-format prints offer detailed views of City Hall, State Street, the Loop, Hull House, Union Station, many other landmarks, circa 1904-1913. Introduction. Captions. Maps. 144pp. 9⅜ x 12¼. 0-486-24656-6

OLD BROOKLYN IN EARLY PHOTOGRAPHS, 1865-1929, William Lee Younger. Luna Park, Gravesend race track, construction of Grand Army Plaza, moving of Hotel Brighton, etc. 157 previously unpublished photographs. 165pp. 8⅞ x 11¾. 0-486-23587-4

THE MYTHS OF THE NORTH AMERICAN INDIANS, Lewis Spence. Rich anthology of the myths and legends of the Algonquins, Iroquois, Pawnees and Sioux, prefaced by an extensive historical and ethnological commentary. 36 illustrations. 480pp. 5⅜ x 8½. 0-486-25967-6

AN ENCYCLOPEDIA OF BATTLES: Accounts of Over 1,560 Battles from 1479 B.C. to the Present, David Eggenberger. Essential details of every major battle in recorded history from the first battle of Megiddo in 1479 B.C. to Grenada in 1984. List of Battle Maps. New Appendix covering the years 1967-1984. Index. 99 illustrations. 544pp. 6½ x 9¼. 0-486-24913-1

SAILING ALONE AROUND THE WORLD, Captain Joshua Slocum. First man to sail around the world, alone, in small boat. One of great feats of seamanship told in delightful manner. 67 illustrations. 294pp. 5⅜ x 8½. 0-486-20326-3

ANARCHISM AND OTHER ESSAYS, Emma Goldman. Powerful, penetrating, prophetic essays on direct action, role of minorities, prison reform, puritan hypocrisy, violence, etc. 271pp. 5⅜ x 8½. 0-486-22484-8

MYTHS OF THE HINDUS AND BUDDHISTS, Ananda K. Coomaraswamy and Sister Nivedita. Great stories of the epics; deeds of Krishna, Shiva, taken from puranas, Vedas, folk tales; etc. 32 illustrations. 400pp. 5⅜ x 8½. 0-486-21759-0

MY BONDAGE AND MY FREEDOM, Frederick Douglass. Born a slave, Douglass became outspoken force in antislavery movement. The best of Douglass' autobiographies. Graphic description of slave life. 464pp. 5⅜ x 8½. 0-486-22457-0

FOLLOWING THE EQUATOR: A Journey Around the World, Mark Twain. Fascinating humorous account of 1897 voyage to Hawaii, Australia, India, New Zealand, etc. Ironic, bemused reports on peoples, customs, climate, flora and fauna, politics, much more. 197 illustrations. 720pp. 5⅜ x 8½. 0-486-26113-1

THE PEOPLE CALLED SHAKERS, Edward D. Andrews. Definitive study of Shakers: origins, beliefs, practices, dances, social organization, furniture and crafts, etc. 33 illustrations. 351pp. 5⅜ x 8½. 0-486-21081-2

THE MYTHS OF GREECE AND ROME, H. A. Guerber. A classic of mythology, generously illustrated, long prized for its simple, graphic, accurate retelling of the principal myths of Greece and Rome, and for its commentary on their origins and significance. With 64 illustrations by Michelangelo, Raphael, Titian, Rubens, Canova, Bernini and others. 480pp. 5⅜ x 8½. 0-486-27584-1

PSYCHOLOGY OF MUSIC, Carl E. Seashore. Classic work discusses music as a medium from psychological viewpoint. Clear treatment of physical acoustics, auditory apparatus, sound perception, development of musical skills, nature of musical feeling, host of other topics. 88 figures. 408pp. 5⅜ x 8½. 0-486-21851-1

LIFE IN ANCIENT EGYPT, Adolf Erman. Fullest, most thorough, detailed older account with much not in more recent books, domestic life, religion, magic, medicine, commerce, much more. Many illustrations reproduce tomb paintings, carvings, hieroglyphs, etc. 597pp. 5⅜ x 8½. 0-486-22632-8

SUNDIALS, Their Theory and Construction, Albert Waugh. Far and away the best, most thorough coverage of ideas, mathematics concerned, types, construction, adjusting anywhere. Simple, nontechnical treatment allows even children to build several of these dials. Over 100 illustrations. 230pp. 5⅜ x 8½. 0-486-22947-5

THEORETICAL HYDRODYNAMICS, L. M. Milne-Thomson. Classic exposition of the mathematical theory of fluid motion, applicable to both hydrodynamics and aerodynamics. Over 600 exercises. 768pp. 6⅛ x 9¼. 0-486-68970-0

OLD-TIME VIGNETTES IN FULL COLOR, Carol Belanger Grafton (ed.). Over 390 charming, often sentimental illustrations, selected from archives of Victorian graphics–pretty women posing, children playing, food, flowers, kittens and puppies, smiling cherubs, birds and butterflies, much more. All copyright-free. 48pp. 9¼ x 12¼. 0-486-27269-9

PERSPECTIVE FOR ARTISTS, Rex Vicat Cole. Depth, perspective of sky and sea, shadows, much more, not usually covered. 391 diagrams, 81 reproductions of drawings and paintings. 279pp. 5⅜ x 8½. 0-486-22487-2

DRAWING THE LIVING FIGURE, Joseph Sheppard. Innovative approach to artistic anatomy focuses on specifics of surface anatomy, rather than muscles and bones. Over 170 drawings of live models in front, back and side views, and in widely varying poses. Accompanying diagrams. 177 illustrations. Introduction. Index. 144pp. 8⅜ x11¼. 0-486-26723-7

GOTHIC AND OLD ENGLISH ALPHABETS: 100 Complete Fonts, Dan X. Solo. Add power, elegance to posters, signs, other graphics with 100 stunning copyright-free alphabets: Blackstone, Dolbey, Germania, 97 more–including many lower-case, numerals, punctuation marks. 104pp. 8⅛ x 11. 0-486-24695-7

THE BOOK OF WOOD CARVING, Charles Marshall Sayers. Finest book for beginners discusses fundamentals and offers 34 designs. "Absolutely first rate . . . well thought out and well executed."–E. J. Tangerman. 118pp. 7¾ x 10⅝. 0-486-23654-4

ILLUSTRATED CATALOG OF CIVIL WAR MILITARY GOODS: Union Army Weapons, Insignia, Uniform Accessories, and Other Equipment, Schuyler, Hartley, and Graham. Rare, profusely illustrated 1846 catalog includes Union Army uniform and dress regulations, arms and ammunition, coats, insignia, flags, swords, rifles, etc. 226 illustrations. 160pp. 9 x 12. 0-486-24939-5

WOMEN'S FASHIONS OF THE EARLY 1900s: An Unabridged Republication of "New York Fashions, 1909," National Cloak & Suit Co. Rare catalog of mail-order fashions documents women's and children's clothing styles shortly after the turn of the century. Captions offer full descriptions, prices. Invaluable resource for fashion, costume historians. Approximately 725 illustrations. 128pp. 8⅜ x 11¼. 0-486-27276-1

HOW TO DO BEADWORK, Mary White. Fundamental book on craft from simple projects to five-bead chains and woven works. 106 illustrations. 142pp. 5⅜ x 8.
0-486-20697-1

THE 1912 AND 1915 GUSTAV STICKLEY FURNITURE CATALOGS, Gustav Stickley. With over 200 detailed illustrations and descriptions, these two catalogs are essential reading and reference materials and identification guides for Stickley furniture. Captions cite materials, dimensions and prices. 112pp. 6½ x 9¼. 0-486-26676-1

EARLY AMERICAN LOCOMOTIVES, John H. White, Jr. Finest locomotive engravings from early 19th century: historical (1804–74), main-line (after 1870), special, foreign, etc. 147 plates. 142pp. 11⅜ x 8¼. 0-486-22772-3

LITTLE BOOK OF EARLY AMERICAN CRAFTS AND TRADES, Peter Stockham (ed.). 1807 children's book explains crafts and trades: baker, hatter, cooper, potter, and many others. 23 copperplate illustrations. 140pp. 4⅝ x 6.
0-486-23336-7

VICTORIAN FASHIONS AND COSTUMES FROM HARPER'S BAZAR, 1867–1898, Stella Blum (ed.). Day costumes, evening wear, sports clothes, shoes, hats, other accessories in over 1,000 detailed engravings. 320pp. 9⅜ x 12¼.
0-486-22990-4

THE LONG ISLAND RAIL ROAD IN EARLY PHOTOGRAPHS, Ron Ziel. Over 220 rare photos, informative text document origin (1844) and development of rail service on Long Island. Vintage views of early trains, locomotives, stations, passengers, crews, much more. Captions. 8⅞ x 11¾. 0-486-26301-0

VOYAGE OF THE LIBERDADE, Joshua Slocum. Great 19th-century mariner's thrilling, first-hand account of the wreck of his ship off South America, the 35-foot boat he built from the wreckage, and its remarkable voyage home. 128pp. 5⅜ x 8½.
0-486-40022-0

TEN BOOKS ON ARCHITECTURE, Vitruvius. The most important book ever written on architecture. Early Roman aesthetics, technology, classical orders, site selection, all other aspects. Morgan translation. 331pp. 5⅜ x 8½. 0-486-20645-9

THE HUMAN FIGURE IN MOTION, Eadweard Muybridge. More than 4,500 stopped-action photos, in action series, showing undraped men, women, children jumping, lying down, throwing, sitting, wrestling, carrying, etc. 390pp. 7⅞ x 10⅝.
0-486-20204-6 Clothbd.

TREES OF THE EASTERN AND CENTRAL UNITED STATES AND CANADA, William M. Harlow. Best one-volume guide to 140 trees. Full descriptions, woodlore, range, etc. Over 600 illustrations. Handy size. 288pp. 4½ x 6⅜. 0-486-20395-6

GROWING AND USING HERBS AND SPICES, Milo Miloradovich. Versatile handbook provides all the information needed for cultivation and use of all the herbs and spices available in North America. 4 illustrations. Index. Glossary. 236pp. 5⅜ x 8½.
0-486-25058-X

BIG BOOK OF MAZES AND LABYRINTHS, Walter Shepherd. 50 mazes and labyrinths in all–classical, solid, ripple, and more–in one great volume. Perfect inexpensive puzzler for clever youngsters. Full solutions. 112pp. 8⅛ x 11. 0-486-22951-3

PIANO TUNING, J. Cree Fischer. Clearest, best book for beginner, amateur. Simple repairs, raising dropped notes, tuning by easy method of flattened fifths. No previous skills needed. 4 illustrations. 201pp. 5⅜ x 8½. 0-486-23267-0

HINTS TO SINGERS, Lillian Nordica. Selecting the right teacher, developing confidence, overcoming stage fright, and many other important skills receive thoughtful discussion in this indispensible guide, written by a world-famous diva of four decades' experience. 96pp. 5⅜ x 8½. 0-486-40094-8

THE COMPLETE NONSENSE OF EDWARD LEAR, Edward Lear. All nonsense limericks, zany alphabets, Owl and Pussycat, songs, nonsense botany, etc., illustrated by Lear. Total of 320pp. 5⅜ x 8½. (Available in U.S. only.) 0-486-20167-8

VICTORIAN PARLOUR POETRY: An Annotated Anthology, Michael R. Turner. 117 gems by Longfellow, Tennyson, Browning, many lesser-known poets. "The Village Blacksmith," "Curfew Must Not Ring Tonight," "Only a Baby Small," dozens more, often difficult to find elsewhere. Index of poets, titles, first lines. xxiii + 325pp. 5⅝ x 8¼. 0-486-27044-0

DUBLINERS, James Joyce. Fifteen stories offer vivid, tightly focused observations of the lives of Dublin's poorer classes. At least one, "The Dead," is considered a masterpiece. Reprinted complete and unabridged from standard edition. 160pp. 5$\frac{3}{16}$ x 8¼. 0-486-26870-5

GREAT WEIRD TALES: 14 Stories by Lovecraft, Blackwood, Machen and Others, S. T. Joshi (ed.). 14 spellbinding tales, including "The Sin Eater," by Fiona McLeod, "The Eye Above the Mantel," by Frank Belknap Long, as well as renowned works by R. H. Barlow, Lord Dunsany, Arthur Machen, W. C. Morrow and eight other masters of the genre. 256pp. 5⅜ x 8½. (Available in U.S. only.) 0-486-40436-6

THE BOOK OF THE SACRED MAGIC OF ABRAMELIN THE MAGE, translated by S. MacGregor Mathers. Medieval manuscript of ceremonial magic. Basic document in Aleister Crowley, Golden Dawn groups. 268pp. 5⅜ x 8½. 0-486-23211-5

THE BATTLES THAT CHANGED HISTORY, Fletcher Pratt. Eminent historian profiles 16 crucial conflicts, ancient to modern, that changed the course of civilization. 352pp. 5⅜ x 8½. 0-486-41129-X

NEW RUSSIAN-ENGLISH AND ENGLISH-RUSSIAN DICTIONARY, M. A. O'Brien. This is a remarkably handy Russian dictionary, containing a surprising amount of information, including over 70,000 entries. 366pp. 4½ x 6⅛. 0-486-20208-9

NEW YORK IN THE FORTIES, Andreas Feininger. 162 brilliant photographs by the well-known photographer, formerly with *Life* magazine. Commuters, shoppers, Times Square at night, much else from city at its peak. Captions by John von Hartz. 181pp. 9¼ x 10¾. 0-486-23585-8

INDIAN SIGN LANGUAGE, William Tomkins. Over 525 signs developed by Sioux and other tribes. Written instructions and diagrams. Also 290 pictographs. 111pp. 6⅛ x 9¼. 0-486-22029-X

ANATOMY: A Complete Guide for Artists, Joseph Sheppard. A master of figure drawing shows artists how to render human anatomy convincingly. Over 460 illustrations. 224pp. 8⅜ x 11¼. 0-486-27279-6

MEDIEVAL CALLIGRAPHY: Its History and Technique, Marc Drogin. Spirited history, comprehensive instruction manual covers 13 styles (ca. 4th century through 15th). Excellent photographs; directions for duplicating medieval techniques with modern tools. 224pp. 8⅜ x 11¼. 0-486-26142-5

DRIED FLOWERS: How to Prepare Them, Sarah Whitlock and Martha Rankin. Complete instructions on how to use silica gel, meal and borax, perlite aggregate, sand and borax, glycerine and water to create attractive permanent flower arrangements. 12 illustrations. 32pp. 5⅜ x 8½. 0-486-21802-3

EASY-TO-MAKE BIRD FEEDERS FOR WOODWORKERS, Scott D. Campbell. Detailed, simple-to-use guide for designing, constructing, caring for and using feeders. Text, illustrations for 12 classic and contemporary designs. 96pp. 5⅜ x 8½. 0-486-25847-5

THE COMPLETE BOOK OF BIRDHOUSE CONSTRUCTION FOR WOOD-WORKERS, Scott D. Campbell. Detailed instructions, illustrations, tables. Also data on bird habitat and instinct patterns. Bibliography. 3 tables. 63 illustrations in 15 figures. 48pp. 5¼ x 8½. 0-486-24407-5

SCOTTISH WONDER TALES FROM MYTH AND LEGEND, Donald A. Mackenzie. 16 lively tales tell of giants rumbling down mountainsides, of a magic wand that turns stone pillars into warriors, of gods and goddesses, evil hags, powerful forces and more. 240pp. 5⅜ x 8½. 0-486-29677-6

THE HISTORY OF UNDERCLOTHES, C. Willett Cunnington and Phyllis Cunnington. Fascinating, well-documented survey covering six centuries of English undergarments, enhanced with over 100 illustrations: 12th-century laced-up bodice, footed long drawers (1795), 19th-century bustles, 19th-century corsets for men, Victorian "bust improvers," much more. 272pp. 5⅜ x 8¼. 0-486-27124-2

ARTS AND CRAFTS FURNITURE: The Complete Brooks Catalog of 1912, Brooks Manufacturing Co. Photos and detailed descriptions of more than 150 now very collectible furniture designs from the Arts and Crafts movement depict davenports, settees, buffets, desks, tables, chairs, bedsteads, dressers and more, all built of solid, quarter-sawed oak. Invaluable for students and enthusiasts of antiques, Americana and the decorative arts. 80pp. 6½ x 9¼. 0-486-27471-3

WILBUR AND ORVILLE: A Biography of the Wright Brothers, Fred Howard. Definitive, crisply written study tells the full story of the brothers' lives and work. A vividly written biography, unparalleled in scope and color, that also captures the spirit of an extraordinary era. 560pp. 6⅛ x 9¼. 0-486-40297-5

THE ARTS OF THE SAILOR: Knotting, Splicing and Ropework, Hervey Garrett Smith. Indispensable shipboard reference covers tools, basic knots and useful hitches; handsewing and canvas work, more. Over 100 illustrations. Delightful reading for sea lovers. 256pp. 5⅜ x 8½. 0-486-26440-8

FRANK LLOYD WRIGHT'S FALLINGWATER: The House and Its History, Second, Revised Edition, Donald Hoffmann. A total revision—both in text and illustrations—of the standard document on Fallingwater, the boldest, most personal architectural statement of Wright's mature years, updated with valuable new material from the recently opened Frank Lloyd Wright Archives. "Fascinating"—*The New York Times.* 116 illustrations. 128pp. 9¼ x 10¾. 0-486-27430-6

PHOTOGRAPHIC SKETCHBOOK OF THE CIVIL WAR, Alexander Gardner. 100 photos taken on field during the Civil War. Famous shots of Manassas Harper's Ferry, Lincoln, Richmond, slave pens, etc. 244pp. 10⅝ x 8¼. 0-486-22731-6

FIVE ACRES AND INDEPENDENCE, Maurice G. Kains. Great back-to-the-land classic explains basics of self-sufficient farming. The one book to get. 95 illustrations. 397pp. 5⅜ x 8½. 0-486-20974-1

A MODERN HERBAL, Margaret Grieve. Much the fullest, most exact, most useful compilation of herbal material. Gigantic alphabetical encyclopedia, from aconite to zedoary, gives botanical information, medical properties, folklore, economic uses, much else. Indispensable to serious reader. 161 illustrations. 888pp. 6½ x 9¼. 2-vol. set. (Available in U.S. only.) Vol. I: 0-486-22798-7 Vol. II: 0-486-22799-5

HIDDEN TREASURE MAZE BOOK, Dave Phillips. Solve 34 challenging mazes accompanied by heroic tales of adventure. Evil dragons, people-eating plants, blood-thirsty giants, many more dangerous adversaries lurk at every twist and turn. 34 mazes, stories, solutions. 48pp. 8¼ x 11. 0-486-24566-7

LETTERS OF W. A. MOZART, Wolfgang A. Mozart. Remarkable letters show bawdy wit, humor, imagination, musical insights, contemporary musical world; includes some letters from Leopold Mozart. 276pp. 5⅜ x 8½. 0-486-22859-2

BASIC PRINCIPLES OF CLASSICAL BALLET, Agrippina Vaganova. Great Russian theoretician, teacher explains methods for teaching classical ballet. 118 illustrations. 175pp. 5⅜ x 8½. 0-486-22036-2

THE JUMPING FROG, Mark Twain. Revenge edition. The original story of The Celebrated Jumping Frog of Calaveras County, a hapless French translation, and Twain's hilarious "retranslation" from the French. 12 illustrations. 66pp. 5⅜ x 8½. 0-486-22686-7

BEST REMEMBERED POEMS, Martin Gardner (ed.). The 126 poems in this superb collection of 19th- and 20th-century British and American verse range from Shelley's "To a Skylark" to the impassioned "Renascence" of Edna St. Vincent Millay and to Edward Lear's whimsical "The Owl and the Pussycat." 224pp. 5⅜ x 8½. 0-486-27165-X

COMPLETE SONNETS, William Shakespeare. Over 150 exquisite poems deal with love, friendship, the tyranny of time, beauty's evanescence, death and other themes in language of remarkable power, precision and beauty. Glossary of archaic terms. 80pp. 5³⁄₁₆ x 8¼. 0-486-26686-9

HISTORIC HOMES OF THE AMERICAN PRESIDENTS, Second, Revised Edition, Irvin Haas. A traveler's guide to American Presidential homes, most open to the public, depicting and describing homes occupied by every American President from George Washington to George Bush. With visiting hours, admission charges, travel routes. 175 photographs. Index. 160pp. 8¼ x 11. 0-486-26751-2

THE WIT AND HUMOR OF OSCAR WILDE, Alvin Redman (ed.). More than 1,000 ripostes, paradoxes, wisecracks: Work is the curse of the drinking classes; I can resist everything except temptation; etc. 258pp. 5⅜ x 8½. 0-486-20602-5

SHAKESPEARE LEXICON AND QUOTATION DICTIONARY, Alexander Schmidt. Full definitions, locations, shades of meaning in every word in plays and poems. More than 50,000 exact quotations. 1,485pp. 6½ x 9¼. 2-vol. set. Vol. 1: 0-486-22726-X Vol. 2: 0-486-22727-8

SELECTED POEMS, Emily Dickinson. Over 100 best-known, best-loved poems by one of America's foremost poets, reprinted from authoritative early editions. No comparable edition at this price. Index of first lines. 64pp. 5³⁄₁₆ x 8¼. 0-486-26466-1

THE INSIDIOUS DR. FU-MANCHU, Sax Rohmer. The first of the popular mystery series introduces a pair of English detectives to their archnemesis, the diabolical Dr. Fu-Manchu. Flavorful atmosphere, fast-paced action, and colorful characters enliven this classic of the genre. 208pp. 5³⁄₁₆ x 8¼. 0-486-29898-1

THE MALLEUS MALEFICARUM OF KRAMER AND SPRENGER, translated by Montague Summers. Full text of most important witchhunter's "bible," used by both Catholics and Protestants. 278pp. 6⅝ x 10. 0-486-22802-9

SPANISH STORIES/CUENTOS ESPAÑOLES: A Dual-Language Book, Angel Flores (ed.). Unique format offers 13 great stories in Spanish by Cervantes, Borges, others. Faithful English translations on facing pages. 352pp. 5⅜ x 8½.
0-486-25399-6

GARDEN CITY, LONG ISLAND, IN EARLY PHOTOGRAPHS, 1869–1919, Mildred H. Smith. Handsome treasury of 118 vintage pictures, accompanied by carefully researched captions, document the Garden City Hotel fire (1899), the Vanderbilt Cup Race (1908), the first airmail flight departing from the Nassau Boulevard Aerodrome (1911), and much more. 96pp. 8⅞ x 11¾. 0-486-40669-5

OLD QUEENS, N.Y., IN EARLY PHOTOGRAPHS, Vincent F. Seyfried and William Asadorian. Over 160 rare photographs of Maspeth, Jamaica, Jackson Heights, and other areas. Vintage views of DeWitt Clinton mansion, 1939 World's Fair and more. Captions. 192pp. 8⅞ x 11. 0-486-26358-4

CAPTURED BY THE INDIANS: 15 Firsthand Accounts, 1750-1870, Frederick Drimmer. Astounding true historical accounts of grisly torture, bloody conflicts, relentless pursuits, miraculous escapes and more, by people who lived to tell the tale. 384pp. 5⅜ x 8½. 0-486-24901-8

THE WORLD'S GREAT SPEECHES (Fourth Enlarged Edition), Lewis Copeland, Lawrence W. Lamm, and Stephen J. McKenna. Nearly 300 speeches provide public speakers with a wealth of updated quotes and inspiration–from Pericles' funeral oration and William Jennings Bryan's "Cross of Gold Speech" to Malcolm X's powerful words on the Black Revolution and Earl of Spenser's tribute to his sister, Diana, Princess of Wales. 944pp. 5⅜ x 8⅜. 0-486-40903-1

THE BOOK OF THE SWORD, Sir Richard F. Burton. Great Victorian scholar/adventurer's eloquent, erudite history of the "queen of weapons"–from prehistory to early Roman Empire. Evolution and development of early swords, variations (sabre, broadsword, cutlass, scimitar, etc.), much more. 336pp. 6⅛ x 9¼.
0-486-25434-8

AUTOBIOGRAPHY: The Story of My Experiments with Truth, Mohandas K. Gandhi. Boyhood, legal studies, purification, the growth of the Satyagraha (nonviolent protest) movement. Critical, inspiring work of the man responsible for the freedom of India. 480pp. 5⅜ x 8½. (Available in U.S. only.) 0-486-24593-4

CELTIC MYTHS AND LEGENDS, T. W. Rolleston. Masterful retelling of Irish and Welsh stories and tales. Cuchulain, King Arthur, Deirdre, the Grail, many more. First paperback edition. 58 full-page illustrations. 512pp. 5⅜ x 8½. 0-486-26507-2

THE PRINCIPLES OF PSYCHOLOGY, William James. Famous long course complete, unabridged. Stream of thought, time perception, memory, experimental methods; great work decades ahead of its time. 94 figures. 1,391pp. 5⅜ x 8½. 2-vol. set.
Vol. I: 0-486-20381-6   Vol. II: 0-486-20382-4

THE WORLD AS WILL AND REPRESENTATION, Arthur Schopenhauer. Definitive English translation of Schopenhauer's life work, correcting more than 1,000 errors, omissions in earlier translations. Translated by E. F. J. Payne. Total of 1,269pp. 5⅜ x 8½. 2-vol. set.   Vol. 1: 0-486-21761-2   Vol. 2: 0-486-21762-0

MAGIC AND MYSTERY IN TIBET, Madame Alexandra David-Neel. Experiences among lamas, magicians, sages, sorcerers, Bonpa wizards. A true psychic discovery. 32 illustrations. 321pp. 5⅜ x 8½. (Available in U.S. only.) 0-486-22682-4

THE EGYPTIAN BOOK OF THE DEAD, E. A. Wallis Budge. Complete reproduction of Ani's papyrus, finest ever found. Full hieroglyphic text, interlinear transliteration, word-for-word translation, smooth translation. 533pp. 6½ x 9¼.
0-486-21866-X

HISTORIC COSTUME IN PICTURES, Braun & Schneider. Over 1,450 costumed figures in clearly detailed engravings–from dawn of civilization to end of 19th century. Captions. Many folk costumes. 256pp. 8⅜ x 11¾. 0-486-23150-X

MATHEMATICS FOR THE NONMATHEMATICIAN, Morris Kline. Detailed, college-level treatment of mathematics in cultural and historical context, with numerous exercises. Recommended Reading Lists. Tables. Numerous figures. 641pp. 5⅜ x 8½.
0-486-24823-2

PROBABILISTIC METHODS IN THE THEORY OF STRUCTURES, Isaac Elishakoff. Well-written introduction covers the elements of the theory of probability from two or more random variables, the reliability of such multivariable structures, the theory of random function, Monte Carlo methods of treating problems incapable of exact solution, and more. Examples. 502pp. 5⅜ x 8½. 0-486-40691-1

THE RIME OF THE ANCIENT MARINER, Gustave Doré, S. T. Coleridge. Doré's finest work; 34 plates capture moods, subtleties of poem. Flawless full-size reproductions printed on facing pages with authoritative text of poem. "Beautiful. Simply beautiful."–*Publisher's Weekly.* 77pp. 9¼ x 12. 0-486-22305-1

SCULPTURE: Principles and Practice, Louis Slobodkin. Step-by-step approach to clay, plaster, metals, stone; classical and modern. 253 drawings, photos. 255pp. 8⅛ x 11.
0-486-22960-2

THE INFLUENCE OF SEA POWER UPON HISTORY, 1660–1783, A. T. Mahan. Influential classic of naval history and tactics still used as text in war colleges. First paperback edition. 4 maps. 24 battle plans. 640pp. 5⅜ x 8½. 0-486-25509-3

THE STORY OF THE TITANIC AS TOLD BY ITS SURVIVORS, Jack Winocour (ed.). What it was really like. Panic, despair, shocking inefficiency, and a little heroism. More thrilling than any fictional account. 26 illustrations. 320pp. 5⅜ x 8½.
0-486-20610-6

ONE TWO THREE . . . INFINITY: Facts and Speculations of Science, George Gamow. Great physicist's fascinating, readable overview of contemporary science: number theory, relativity, fourth dimension, entropy, genes, atomic structure, much more. 128 illustrations. Index. 352pp. 5⅜ x 8½. 0-486-25664-2

DALÍ ON MODERN ART: The Cuckolds of Antiquated Modern Art, Salvador Dalí. Influential painter skewers modern art and its practitioners. Outrageous evaluations of Picasso, Cézanne, Turner, more. 15 renderings of paintings discussed. 44 calligraphic decorations by Dalí. 96pp. 5⅜ x 8½. (Available in U.S. only.) 0-486-29220-7

ANTIQUE PLAYING CARDS: A Pictorial History, Henry René D'Allemagne. Over 900 elaborate, decorative images from rare playing cards (14th–20th centuries): Bacchus, death, dancing dogs, hunting scenes, royal coats of arms, players cheating, much more. 96pp. 9¼ x 12¼. 0-486-29265-7

MAKING FURNITURE MASTERPIECES: 30 Projects with Measured Drawings, Franklin H. Gottshall. Step-by-step instructions, illustrations for constructing handsome, useful pieces, among them a Sheraton desk, Chippendale chair, Spanish desk, Queen Anne table and a William and Mary dressing mirror. 224pp. 8⅛ x 11¼. 0-486-29338-6

NORTH AMERICAN INDIAN DESIGNS FOR ARTISTS AND CRAFTSPEOPLE, Eva Wilson. Over 360 authentic copyright-free designs adapted from Navajo blankets, Hopi pottery, Sioux buffalo hides, more. Geometrics, symbolic figures, plant and animal motifs, etc. 128pp. 8⅜ x 11. (Not for sale in the United Kingdom.) 0-486-25341-4

THE FOSSIL BOOK: A Record of Prehistoric Life, Patricia V. Rich et al. Profusely illustrated definitive guide covers everything from single-celled organisms and dinosaurs to birds and mammals and the interplay between climate and man. Over 1,500 illustrations. 760pp. 7½ x 10⅛. 0-486-29371-8

VICTORIAN ARCHITECTURAL DETAILS: Designs for Over 700 Stairs, Mantels, Doors, Windows, Cornices, Porches, and Other Decorative Elements, A. J. Bicknell & Company. Everything from dormer windows and piazzas to balconies and gable ornaments. Also includes elevations and floor plans for handsome, private residences and commercial structures. 80pp. 9⅜ x 12¼. 0-486-44015-X

WESTERN ISLAMIC ARCHITECTURE: A Concise Introduction, John D. Hoag. Profusely illustrated critical appraisal compares and contrasts Islamic mosques and palaces–from Spain and Egypt to other areas in the Middle East. 139 illustrations. 128pp. 6 x 9. 0-486-43760-4

CHINESE ARCHITECTURE: A Pictorial History, Liang Ssu-ch'eng. More than 240 rare photographs and drawings depict temples, pagodas, tombs, bridges, and imperial palaces comprising much of China's architectural heritage. 152 halftones, 94 diagrams. 232pp. 10¾ x 9⅞. 0-486-43999-2

THE RENAISSANCE: Studies in Art and Poetry, Walter Pater. One of the most talked-about books of the 19th century, *The Renaissance* combines scholarship and philosophy in an innovative work of cultural criticism that examines the achievements of Botticelli, Leonardo, Michelangelo, and other artists. "The holy writ of beauty."–Oscar Wilde. 160pp. 5⅜ x 8½. 0-486-44025-7

A TREATISE ON PAINTING, Leonardo da Vinci. The great Renaissance artist's practical advice on drawing and painting techniques covers anatomy, perspective, composition, light and shadow, and color. A classic of art instruction, it features 48 drawings by Nicholas Poussin and Leon Battista Alberti. 192pp. 5⅜ x 8½. 0-486-44155-5

THE MIND OF LEONARDO DA VINCI, Edward McCurdy. More than just a biography, this classic study by a distinguished historian draws upon Leonardo's extensive writings to offer numerous demonstrations of the Renaissance master's achievements, not only in sculpture and painting, but also in music, engineering, and even experimental aviation. 384pp. 5⅜ x 8½. 0-486-44142-3

WASHINGTON IRVING'S RIP VAN WINKLE, Illustrated by Arthur Rackham. Lovely prints that established artist as a leading illustrator of the time and forever etched into the popular imagination a classic of Catskill lore. 51 full-color plates. 80pp. 8⅜ x 11. 0-486-44242-X

HENSCHE ON PAINTING, John W. Robichaux. Basic painting philosophy and methodology of a great teacher, as expounded in his famous classes and workshops on Cape Cod. 7 illustrations in color on covers. 80pp. 5⅜ x 8½. 0-486-43728-0

LIGHT AND SHADE: A Classic Approach to Three-Dimensional Drawing, Mrs. Mary P. Merrifield. Handy reference clearly demonstrates principles of light and shade by revealing effects of common daylight, sunshine, and candle or artificial light on geometrical solids. 13 plates. 64pp. 5⅜ x 8½. 0-486-44143-1

ASTROLOGY AND ASTRONOMY: A Pictorial Archive of Signs and Symbols, Ernst and Johanna Lehner. Treasure trove of stories, lore, and myth, accompanied by more than 300 rare illustrations of planets, the Milky Way, signs of the zodiac, comets, meteors, and other astronomical phenomena. 192pp. 8⅜ x 11. 0-486-43981-X

JEWELRY MAKING: Techniques for Metal, Tim McCreight. Easy-to-follow instructions and carefully executed illustrations describe tools and techniques, use of gems and enamels, wire inlay, casting, and other topics. 72 line illustrations and diagrams. 176pp. 8¼ x 10⅞. 0-486-44043-5

MAKING BIRDHOUSES: Easy and Advanced Projects, Gladstone Califf. Easy-to-follow instructions include diagrams for everything from a one-room house for bluebirds to a forty-two-room structure for purple martins. 56 plates; 4 figures. 80pp. 8¾ x 6⅜. 0-486-44183-0

LITTLE BOOK OF LOG CABINS: How to Build and Furnish Them, William S. Wicks. Handy how-to manual, with instructions and illustrations for building cabins in the Adirondack style, fireplaces, stairways, furniture, beamed ceilings, and more. 102 line drawings. 96pp. 8¾ x 6⅜. 0-486-44259-4

THE SEASONS OF AMERICA PAST, Eric Sloane. From "sugaring time" and strawberry picking to Indian summer and fall harvest, a whole year's activities described in charming prose and enhanced with 79 of the author's own illustrations. 160pp. 8¼ x 11. 0-486-44220-9

THE METROPOLIS OF TOMORROW, Hugh Ferriss. Generous, prophetic vision of the metropolis of the future, as perceived in 1929. Powerful illustrations of towering structures, wide avenues, and rooftop parks–all features in many of today's modern cities. 59 illustrations. 144pp. 8¼ x 11. 0-486-43727-2

THE PATH TO ROME, Hilaire Belloc. This 1902 memoir abounds in lively vignettes from a vanished time, recounting a pilgrimage on foot across the Alps and Apennines in order to "see all Europe which the Christian Faith has saved." 77 of the author's original line drawings complement his sparkling prose. 272pp. 5⅜ x 8½. 0-486-44001-X

THE HISTORY OF RASSELAS: Prince of Abissinia, Samuel Johnson. Distinguished English writer attacks eighteenth-century optimism and man's unrealistic estimates of what life has to offer. 112pp. 5⅜ x 8½. 0-486-44094-X

A VOYAGE TO ARCTURUS, David Lindsay. A brilliant flight of pure fancy, where wild creatures crowd the fantastic landscape and demented torturers dominate victims with their bizarre mental powers. 272pp. 5⅜ x 8½. 0-486-44198-9

Paperbound unless otherwise indicated. Available at your book dealer, online at **www.doverpublications.com**, or by writing to Dept. GI, Dover Publications, Inc., 31 East 2nd Street, Mineola, NY 11501. For current price information or for free catalogs (please indicate field of interest), write to Dover Publications or log on to **www.doverpublications.com** and see every Dover book in print. Dover publishes more than 500 books each year on science, elementary and advanced mathematics, biology, music, art, literary history, social sciences, and other areas.